I0012932

HOW TO SELF PU
WRITE TODAY – PUBLISH TOMORROW
THE BEST SELF PUBLISHING GUIDE
By James Burton Anderson

Amazon CreateSpace Paperback Edition

ISBN #978-1-893257-62-7   First Edition

Copyright 2012   Lions Pride Publishing Co., LLC

Every effort has been made to make this book as complete and accurate as possible. However, there may be mistakes in typography or content. Also, this book contains information on earning writing

To my beautiful wife Melanie, whose patience and understanding allows me endless hours writing on the computer while she works a demanding 9 to 5 and still keeps our household from falling apart!

And, to the two author-geniuses who have most influenced my writing and publishing over the past decades, Dan Poynter and Dr. Jeffrey Lant, my deepest thanks for their guidance and inspiration.

INDEX

FORWARD

I have been writing and publishing books since 1970. Most of these were published before the "electronic era". One would write a manuscript and submit it for publication to any one of a vast number of publishing houses. If one of these were to accept the manuscript for publication, which was **very** unlikely, you, the struggling and starving author, might possibly get ten percent of the cover price as your "royalty".

If you were not accepted by a publisher, you had the only other choice which was to "self-publish". This necessitated paying up front to have some cost-effective quantity of books printed. You could expect to pay up to ten dollars or so per book depending upon size, length and type of cover, packaging and shipment. To get a decent unit price you would have to print at least a thousand copies. Then you had to market the books yourself. I can say from long and sad experience that it was **VERY** difficult to make a living at this. I can also say that every author I know, myself included, has many cartons of unsold costly "remainder" books sitting in storage somewhere!

Authors today have absolutely no need whatsoever to seek out a major publisher. In fact, I have no idea how or why publishing houses stay in business. We are in the electronic era. More books today are actually downloaded electronically than are purchased as physical books! There certainly is nothing a big publishing house can do for you that you cannot do for yourself, though they would all protest that statement vigorously.

But what about those **physical** books? Don't people still buy them? Yes indeed they do. What has changed the entire face of the publishing industry is the simple fact that no longer do you have to print, store, and ship a quantity of books. Today books can be printed as they are sold, one at a time, **printed on demand!**

On top of that, the royalties paid to authors today by the electronic-publishers run anywhere from 45% to 75%! And the basic marketing is done for FREE by massive billion-dollar retailers such as Amazon! One can actually make a very substantial living today as a totally obscure author. This was utterly impossible as recently as ten years ago, and somewhat difficult even three years ago. **These are _GREAT_ times to be an independent unknown writer!**

There are four key routes to self-publishing success, and it is important to master all four to optimize your profits. Two of these are run by the biggest book retailer on the planet, Amazon, one by Barnes and Noble, and one by a company called Smashwords. As a percentage of overall revenue from these four sources, my experience is 35% from Amazon Kindle Direct Publishing (electronic "eBooks" sold on Kindle devices), 20% from Amazon Create Space (physical books printed on-demand and marketed by Amazon), 10% from Barnes and Noble (electronic NOOK "eBooks"), and 35% from Smashwords other outlets.

Overall, these four amount collectively to about 70% of everything you can earn from your books, the 30% balance being from your own direct sales at your own website.

Smashwords markets eBooks through a number of very important channels. Aside from their own marketing, they sell your works through Apple iBooks, Diesel, SONY, Stanza, Aldiko, Kobo and Nook. They will also do Amazon for you, but I very much prefer to do those directly myself even though it is a lot more work. The reason is higher commissions, and **much** faster payouts, when working directly with Amazon.

Unless you were a writer before the age of computers, you cannot begin to understand the night and day difference this all has made. Today you never have to leave your desk, your den room, or your kitchen table, or even get dressed to be a very successful author! And you can be successful with an absolute minimum of expense. There is a bit to learn, but it is very far from rocket science. Even mediocre books sell well if marketed properly. You do not even have to create your own material!

In the Chapters that follow I will walk you through the steps you need to take to be successful. There is a learning curve, but this book will flatten the curve and save you endless hours of trial and error. Once you publish one single book on each platform, every successive book becomes **easier** to publish. That first one is a small pain in the rear, no matter how much of my knowledge and experience I share with you! Each of the retailers has a totally different way in which your material must be presented. You cannot just write a manuscript and upload it to their respective websites. That would be **too easy!** This is actual work.

Nor can you write a single set of descriptive information about the book, about you the author, or about any of the details required to publish, because every single one of these electronic publishers has quite different file-size requirements and file type requirements from the others. You literally have to look at each one as a totally separate project once you have created your book's manuscript in your word processor.

It is actually very easy to become a self-publisher. It's a job, like any other, but a lot more fun! As I will explain later on in this book, you do not need any particular writing skills, just a determination to earn money from the comfort of your home.

CHAPTER 1
WHY SELF-PUBLISHING?

The secret key to building wealth is knowing things other people do not know and acting upon them. Learn and earn.

In the '40s and '50s my ex-father-in-law was the top earning salesman for a Fortune 500 company selling sheets and pillowcases. He became very wealthy. He daily wore a tie clasp that had the acronym: "YCDBSOYA" on it. It stood for: **Y**ou **C**an't **D**o **B**usiness **S**itting **O**n **Y**our **A**ss". Maybe true then. Not true today!

That was before you **COULD** do business sitting on your duff in front of a computer screen. And in this book I will share what I consider to be the best and easiest way to make as much money as you desire sitting at your keypad in the comfort of your home writing books and reports and self-publishing them to the general public.

During my lifetime there have been very few "culture shifts". Certainly the internet in general is the major culture-shift that comes to mind. Social site interactions on Facebook, MySpace, Twitter, YouTube and Pinterest are a major result of this culture shift. But there is another true culture shift happening today at an incredible pace. <u>This is the shift away from printed books to electronically downloaded eBooks.</u>

A few years ago I was most surprised when I learned that Amazon is drooling over having anyone, you, me, anyone, write books and booklets and articles and reports for them to advertise and publish electronically. They called it <u>"Kindle Direct Publishing"</u> or KDP. Exciting? Hell yes!!!! And you are getting in very nearly on the ground floor.

Every author knows that Amazon sells hard and soft cover books, and know that they can list their books for sale at Amazon.com. But KDP is totally different from selling printed hard and soft cover books (and even ebooks) through Amazon.com's regular book-selling site. **KDP is an entity unto itself.**

The reading "Tablet", led by Amazon's "Kindle" and its latest iterations (e.g., "Kindle Fire") are found and used everywhere. It is reported that in excess of 20 tablet readers are sold every minute!

As Robin Williams popularized in *Dead Poets Society*, "**CARPE DIEM**". Sieze the Day! This ebook phenomenon, this culture shift following hundreds of years of printed book reading, has created an incredible opportunity for the internet self-publisher that cannot be overlooked or understated. This culture shift can be your key to lifetime riches.

You are on the cutting edge of something **HUGE**. In terms of dollars, and in terms of the number of Best Selling Titles, ebooks are rapidly pulling away from printed books.

You will see e-readers everywhere. People use them lying in bed, sitting on the crapper, on the beach, commuting, while watching TV, in classes and meetings, or waiting on supermarket lines!

Amazon sells one million Kindles a week, and loses money on every one of them. But as with Gillette giving away razors to sell razor blades years ago, all Amazon cares about is the money they can earn selling eBooks….**YOUR** ebooks! The ebook market is reported to be between $2 and $3 BILLION annually!

In Amazon we have a multi-billion dollar world-renowned corporation promoting **your** virtual product for FREE and paying you handsomely for the privilege! Sounds too good to be true? Believe me, it's true!

Amazon is one of the world's most successful companies. I never cease to be amazed that I can order a printed book from Amazon today and have it delivered to my doorstep within two days at half the price it would cost me at my local bookstore! Indeed, most people think of Amazon only as an "on-line book store", and rightly so. That's what they are. I know always thought of them in that light.

But Amazon is <u>much</u> more than that. For example, one can sell items in Amazon auctions much as they do on eBay. I find eBay quite adequate for my needs, but I know a number of internet entrepreneurs who successfully sell in Amazon auctions as well.

So now we have the Amazon "Kindle", that flat little piece of electronic gadgetry that Oprah Winfrey went bonkers over a few years ago. You buy it, and can read books that are pre-programmed on it. Then using it you can buy just about any book you could imagine, and download it to be read on the Kindle device whenever and wherever.

There is no limit to the number of books it will store because, unlike the iPad, it does not depend on internal storage. Everything is downloaded via cell phone towers, and stored permanently on Amazon's "cloud" servers. Pretty cool.

What I was very surprised to learn is that the Kindle-ready ebooks can also be purchased and downloaded on **ANY** digital device. On desktops and laptops. On cell phones and even on some gaming devices.   They have applications (apps) for iPads and Blackberries. So you don't have to buy the Kindle Tablet thingie at all. This means that your potential customer base is in the hundreds of millions, a pure "numbers game". Heck, I don't need a small slice of the Kindle-universe pie. I just want to lick the knife. Even a small lick will suffice!

Latest statistics show that books delivered electronically, "ebook" sales, reportedly passed print book sales in 2010. This is pretty remarkable when you consider that ebooks have only been around for a decade or so. The printing press pre-dates the internet by a few millennia! **This is a true culture shift. It is up to you to take full advantage of it.**

THE SUCCESS TEMPLATE

At first it will take much longer to post any item to your Kindle or other self-publishing account . You will find that each successive effort takes less time. This is because you will develop a "template" mentality. You have a multi-part "template" that you repeat over and over and over, as follows:

First you find a niche of "starving" buyers.

Do your keyword research, as explained in

Chapter 11. You will be doing exactly the same sort of keyword search you would do to optimize a website.

Create a killer title. (Try to match your title to an EXACT keyword search term for maximum sales.)

Create a killer cover;

Create killer descriptions;

Create your masterpiece (i.e., book);
Price your book;

Last, Upload to your self-publishing accounts. The upload process can take many minutes; do not get worried or impatient while items are accepted into the various platforms.

Employ one or more of the marketing techniques explained in Chapters 17 to 25.

These are the most important general aspects of self- publishing.   Content can be mediocre (most of what sells well is far from great) but if these steps are done correctly regardless of quality you can sell lots of books. Ignore the importance of these steps and you could write Pulitzer Prize material and never sell a copy.

PROMOTION TRICKS OF THE TRADE

Posting favorable reviews of your work is important. You should be able to get favorable reviews from friends, family and associates. You can also go to go to fiverr.com and actually <u>pay</u> someone to write a favorable review for five bucks! Personally I consider this to be highly unethical, but your competition will probably be using it so you decide how you want to proceed.

The least ethical way is to pay five bucks to a person at fiverr.com, write your five-star review for them, and they post it! It's done every day. Better is where you buy your book for them, they hopefully actually read it, and post a review that they wrote themselves. Of course, because they want repeat business, these reviews tend to be something less than honest!

Join some Kindle and other self-publisher forums. Check out ereadforum.net and kindleboards.com. You can add a link to your book in your forum signature, or even a website link to some free offer relevant to the content of your book. Follow some of the other KDP authors' blogs and reply strings. You can learn a lot. Eventually start your own blog.

Unless your ego rules your pocketbook, it is a good idea to use a different pen name as the author of **each** book you create, at least for non-fiction works. Pen names and ghostwriters are used throughout the publishing industry (not to mention Hollywood) and are perfectly ethical and legal. The reason for this, in the case of non-fiction books, is that no single author could credibly be an expert whose advice on a vast variety of topics should be followed. Unless your name is Leonardo da Vinci!

Always end your price with "7". Deviate from this at your peril!

Split-test everything. Try different prices. Try different Titles. Try different covers. Try different descriptions. Try substituting a male pen name for a female one (I always start out with a female pen name. For whatever reason it pulls mare sales over the exact same item with a male pen name.) Most highly successful KPD marketers I know split test as often as possible.

Load up your Title and Description with keywords relevant to the information in your ebook.

Be certain to create an eye-catching cover. **This is critical. Covers sell books.**

Create QUALITY books. In the long run it trumps "easily created QUANTITY of crap" every time.

Writing and self-publishing is a lot easier than you probably think. The hardest part is getting started. Read this book, lay aside your fears, and **JUST DO IT!**

CHAPTER 2

<u>OVERVIEW – THE FOUR BASIC PLATFORMS</u>

There are four basic self-publishing platforms that I have used successfully. There may be others, and more will surely be created in the future. Self-publishing **is** the future. One can see evidence of this in the recent purchase by huge Penguin Books, a traditional publishing house, of a self-publishing company.

There are three basic formats in which you will be selling your books are: electronically downloaded on various devices; print-on-demand; and downloadable .pdf files. **You can cover the first of these with accounts at Amazon Kindle Direct Publishing and Smashwords. Amazon Create Space is the print-on-demand platform. Your own website sells .pdf downloadable copies.**

What complicates matters greatly is that each of these four platforms requires somewhat different elements.

There are seven elements to consider: the cover (front/spine/back); the barcode; the ISBN number; the book text upload; the text description; about the author; and the locator tags.

I strongly suggest you print a copy of the following information and keep it handy. I also suggest that you prepare ALL of the required material BEFORE you upload anything to any of the publishing platforms. You will be amazed at how much this will facilitate getting everything uploaded with a minimum of confusion.

AMAZON KINDLE:

COVER: Not strictly required, but absolutely essential because "the cover sells the book". Upload as .jpeg or .tiff file. Minimum 1,000 pixels on the long side, 1.6:1.0 size ratio (625 pixels short side).

BARCODE: Not required.

ISBN #: Not required. You, however, already will have one designated for an ebook for your Smashwords Premium Catalog account, so you might as well use it.

TEXT: Special .prc file with "clickable" table of contents.

You could upload other file types, but ebook-reader users want to click on a table of contents to move through the book, and you will get many book returns without a clickable table of contents.

TEXT DESCRIPTION: 4,000 characters maximum (spaces count as characters).

ABOUT AUTHOR: 2,500 characters maximim (spaces count as characters).

LOCATOR TAGS (KEYWORD PHRASES): maximum of seven, each less than twenty five characters/spaces.

SMASHWORDS:

COVER: .jpeg or .png file, 20mb maximum. 1,400 pixels wide x 2,100 pixels high (for a 6" x 9" book).

BARCODE: Not required.

ISBN #: Not required for some distribution channels, but a must for Apple, SONY, and KOBO e-readers. You will need to buy one from Bowker. Smashwords will supply one for $9.95, but they will be shown as the publisher.

TEXT: Upload .doc file ONLY, not .docx or .pdf. Maximum 5mb. If you want distribution to the Premium Catalog (**and you do**) you MUST have a very unique formatting in accordance with a massive "Smashwords Style Guide".

TEXT DESCRIPTIONS: SHORT: 400 characters. Long: 4,000 characters (spaces count as characters).

ABOUT AUTHOR: No size limitations stated.

LOCATOR TAGS (KEYWORD PHRASES): Unlimited, any length.

AMAZON CREATE SPACE (Print-on-demand):

NOTE: You will need two separate files, one specifically for library distribution, the first with your own ISBN# (if you so choose) the library edition with a mandatory Amazon ISBN#.

COVER: Upload as a .pdf file. Cover must have back/spine/front, and be designed for a specific size book.

BARCODE: Required, but Amazon creates one for free. You need to leave space for it on the back cover lower right corner.

ISBN #: Required. Four options, detailed on their site: Free, $10.00, $99.00, or "you provide". The difference is in who is listed as publisher (I prefer it be me or my company for "branding" purposes) and what distribution channels are made available. The free version, and the one you provide, open up all distribution channels.

TEXT: 400mb maximum. Can be .docx, .doc, or .pdf. It is definitely preferable to write in MS WORD, create the page size for the book size you want, convert it to a .pdf, check your formatting, and upload it in that .pdf format. It saves a great deal of time and trouble.

TEXT DESCRIPTION: 5,000 characters maximum (spaces count as characters).

ABOUT AUTHOR: 2,500 characters maximum (spaces count as characters).

LOCATOR TAGS (KEYWORD PHRASES): Maximum of five, any length.

YOUR OWN WEBSITE:

COVER: No limitations. Can be two-dimensional as used in Kindle and Smashwords, or created as three-dimensional.

BARCODE: Not applicable.

ISBN #: Not strictly required, though I prefer using a unique one.

TEXT: As a .pdf downloadable upon visitor payment.

TEXT DESCRIPTION: Unlimited length sales page.

ABOUT AUTHOR: Unlimited length page.

LOCATOR TAGS (KEYWORD PHRASES): Used as meta-tags and within the text.

NEEDED FOR THE REAR COVER OF A 6 X 9 BOOK:

ABOUT THE AUTHOR: Approximately 110 words.

ABOUT THE BOOK: Approximately 170 words

TESTIMONIALS: Two lines, approximately ten words each.

TEASER COPY: Approximately eight words.

PATH TO FIND BOOK: Primary and secondary.

LOGO

BARCODE, provided free by Amazon Create Space.

NEEDED TO BUY AN ISBN # AT BOWKER:

COVER: Upload as .jpeg file, 4kb – 5kb size.

BARCODE: Not applicable.

ISBN #: Imbed in the book's title page to relate to the ISBN # you are buying from them.

TEXT: Upload as .pdf, with the specific ISBN number purchased for that version of your book (i.e. Kindle edition, Smashword edition, or Create Space edition) on the title page.

TEXT DESCRIPTION: 350 words maximum.

ABOUT AUTHOR: 350 words maximum.

LOCATOR TAGS (KEYWORD PHRASES): Not applicable.

As you can see from the above you will need to write various length versions of the same things. I strongly suggest, as earlier mentioned, that you write every possible version before you open **any** of the above accounts. If you try to do this by completing one platform, and then going to the next one, you will find that the publication process gets very confusing, and will be stretched out over a much longer time period.

This is not as complicated as it may seem looking at the above. Here is an overall summary of the elements I create:

ABOUT THE BOOK: Three files, 170 words, 350 words, 4,000 characters.

ABOUT THE AUTHOR: Three files, 110 words, 2,500 characters, and unlimited (for the book itself).

KEYWORDS: Find the top ten in terms of traffic. Then continue search until you find a total of seven that have under 25 characters.

ISBN #: I buy four for each book (Kindle, Smashwords, Create Space, and my website.)

COVER: One 2-dimensional, One 3-dimensional (optional, for website); One back/spine/front cover sized for the specific book size and thickness.

Once you have all of the above material ready to upload, you can do Kindle, Create

Space and Smashwords entirely within about two hours or less! The website is a different matter, and you may not even want to have one, but it is a very important component of your overall marketing strategy.

Here are some classical old-time marketing truisms. People are motivated by a very small set of human needs (in no particular order):

The need to relieve pain, physical or psychological;
The desire for wealth;

The desire to have people like them, personal acceptance;
The desire for health and longevity;
The desire for happiness, with one's self and in relationships (The shrinks call this "self-actualization");
The desire for knowledge.

Whatever ebook or report or article you create it must in some way <u>address one of these human needs</u>.

To the best of my knowledge there is no other report other than the one you are reading that offers you the complete marketing training offered below. Read on and prosper!

The basic steps that are common to each project you create are:

Decide on your business type, (sole proprietor, C-corp, LLC, etc) and register locally if required by law;
Get multiple free email accounts (Yahoo! mail or Google gmail), ten recommended.
Get a logo for you or your business;
Write your manuscript, fiction or non-fiction;
Carefully proof-read and make all corrections;
Chose a title;
Decide on who will be the author and publisher;

Buy four ISBN numbers from Bowker (our use free ones);

Create a list of keywords;

Write a copyright and disclaimer page;

Write a dedication;

Create an Index, with pages un-numbered;

Study a general list of "power words" and insert them;

Write descriptions of the manuscript;

Write "About The Author" descriptions;

Create a two-dimensional front-side book cover;

Create a rear-side book cover and spine;

Get a FREE PayPal business account;

Join each of the book publishers; it's FREE;

Get your manuscript converted into the accepted formats;

Upload your manuscripts to the publishers;

Upload your cover and other required details;

Choose your pricing;

Choose how you will be paid;

Obtain a relevant domain name;

Create a mini-website;

Market aggressively;

Sit back and collect royalties!

I will cover each of these steps in detail throughout this book.

Next, there are many marketing steps you must follow to insure that your book sells well. The more of these you pursue the more you will earn. You can greatly multiply your revenue by focusing on all of the following marketing steps together. These include:

Outsourcing to Fiverr;
Press releases, free and paid;
Articles sent to article directories, free & paid;
An eBay store;
A CraigsList account;
A blog;
Forum participation;
Social media participation;
Online classified ads, free and paid;
E-Newsletter ads;
Conventional off-line advertising;

Organic website traffic;
Google AdWords pay-per-click traffic.

You can do 100% of the above entirely on your own, **OR**, you can outsource almost all of it for far less cost than you might imagine.

In the Chapters that follow I will share with you all of the information **that will save you hundreds of hours of frustration and aggravation.** I will also share what I have learned in each step of your post-manuscript writing, most of which is anything but intuitive. Learn from my mistakes. Don't try to reinvent the wheel.

If you are a "teckie" and really know every nuance of your computer and word processor you will have a major leg up on non-teckies such as me. I'm a writer. I am not particularly computer literate. Yet I have become very proficient in getting my stuff published quickly. You may very well develop your own shortcuts over time.

Again, it isn't rocket science, just a bit confusing at first.

Each of the electronic publishers has **extensive tutorials** on their websites, extensive videos, answers to common questions, and user forums. They are time consuming to watch, and some are difficult to digest. Follow my simple how-to instructions in this book and save yourself a lot of learning-time.

<u>One very strong word of advice.</u> Do NOT **<u>ever</u>** try to work on more than one book at a time. You will end up in a padded cell, on drugs, or in an AA class! It is extremely difficult to keep everything straight and organized working on just one single book at a time. There is a strong inverse economy of scale! Finish one book, every publisher platform, every step, all marketing, **<u>then and only then</u>** go on to the next book. This is one piece of advice for which you will thank me later!

CHAPTER 3

<u>CREATING YOUR MASTERPIECE</u>

Obviously, the most important thing you need to do to do is to create the actual product itself, your report or book. From a time standpoint the actual writing is only about half of the entire process of creating and selling your masterpiece The preliminaries above, plus your post-publication marketing, are FAR more important. A lot of weak copy is sold with a great cover, title and description, and expert marketing.

There are four ways to create your book. Writing from scratch, using the Public Domain, buying Private Label Rights, and paying a ghostwriter.

It is unlikely that you are a professional writer. You may not even be a good writer. But for some, the easiest, fastest and cheapest way is to simply write from personal experience. Write about things you know well. Write about your personal passions. Write about life experiences.

Remember, your material isn't being read by your High School English teacher. The chances are that anything you write is being read by an average individual with limited detailed knowledge of technical English. It is fact is that very few individuals are capable writers.

The good news is that **you do not have to actually write anything original yourself!** (It would save you some time and money if you or a relative or friend could string together sentences that make sense, but even that isn't needed). With computer "spell check" you don't even need to be able to spell! If I had a dollar for every word I misspell while writing a given book I wouldn't need to sell any!

Below I will explain ways you can create a book or report that individuals will buy and that requires no writing on your part at all. One is free (or almost free) and takes a serious amount of work. The other two cost some bucks but are very easy.

FREE CONTENT – PUBLIC DOMAIN MATERIAL

The free way to obtain written material is to access the Public Domain. This can be anything written that is not under current copyright. The simplest way to do this is to go to a used book store, or to a website (such as abebooks.com) and buy anything copyrighted before 1922.

For example, I bought a beat up old 1899 book of "Myths For Children". I copy each chapter exactly, and sell each chapter as a childrens' ebook. There were ten chapters. Voila! Ten profitable ebooks. You could buy old romance novels, poetry books, recipe books, you name it. Then write a great title, a great description, create a great cover, copy it all into "Word", and upload it to to one of the publishing platforms.

You can also do Google searches for public domain articles and combine them in a unique fashion to create a product. Most of what the US government publishes is not copyrighted. You can find countless government publications on almost any subject imaginable.

Copying anything in the public domain manually might take a while, unless you are a very rapid typist. To this day I am a "one finger" typist, so I prefer either of two other ways to go. I bought a software program called "Dragon Naturally Speaking". It wasn't cheap, but it is a massive time saver. I simply read the book content into a microphone and it magically appears in "Word"! It is about 99% accurate, so I do need to go over it once for minor corrections, but overall it saves me many hours of typing.

Another way to copy a book onto a computer is with a scanner and an Optical Character Recognition (OCR) software program. It is quite effective depending upon the clarity and size of the book I am copying.

If you choose to use Public Domain material make certain that someone else (or many someone elses!) are not using the same material. This is a quick way to get tossed off any publishing site. Doing some in-depth search should be able to determine with some degree of certainty that you are offering a unique item.

Your best success route is to make significant changes in any of the Public Domain material. Rewording, combining reports on similar topics, or best of all learning the material and publishing it in your own words.

ALMOST FREE CONTENT – PRIVATE LABEL RIGHTS

Aside from Public Domain items, there is another option. This is the buying of "Private Label Rights" articles known in the trade as "PLR". The easiest way to do this is to go to any of the many sites that sell these rights. I use two: theplrstore.com and master-resale-rights.com

You can buy an endless variety of material for $2.99 to $9.99. Some you _must_ re-publish with no changes per the license granted. **Avoid this material.** To most of the PLR material you can add your name or a pen name as the author, and make any changes you might care to make in the copy.

Remember, however, that you do not have exclusive rights to PLR material. Someone else is probably buying the same stuff. This is where your creativity must win the day. And this is where you can get into **BIG** trouble with Amazon, orr any publishing platform.

For example, Amazon wants its Kindle users to buy only quality material. When they see the same PLR material, even with some minor changes, used over and over by different authors you will definitely get "Kindle Slapped". Your material will be removed, and you can be banned from Kindle forever. Personally, I'm not real fond of rejection. They will reject anything that looks similar to some other offering in the system. This is also true of Smashwords.

You must look at all PLR material as **research**. If you find a dozen or so articles on a topic, read them, put them aside, and then write a totally unique piece that summarizes the material, you have created an acceptable item.

Resist the temptation to load up your publishing accounts with crappy PLR material, stuff you copy almost exactly. It's fast and easy, but 100% fruitless and self-defeating. You want quality over quantity. This will make you much more money in the long run and keep you in good stead with Amazon and Smashwords. They DO review all of your material before approving it for publication. And they DO compare it with everything else that is in their system. And you **WILL** get caught.

Because of the well –publicized "Kindle Slap of 2011" you would be well advised to entirely avoid PLR and PD material altogether, unless you are a very clever re-writer. That is, only if you care whether you are thrown off the platforms permanently. You really don't want that.

The days of trying to sell non-original content are over. Use this stuff as reference material only. Amazon, as does Google, HATES duplicate content. They want their visitors to have quality visits and buy quality ebooks. You can't blame them. By "reference material" I don't mean change a word or two here and there. But If you are capable of doing the needed a 99% re-write of PLR or PD material then you might as well write new material from scratch. And you can always pay someone else to write for you.

THE UN-FREE CONTENT - HIRING A FREELANCER

The last, and most expensive way to create your book is to pay a professional freelance writer. Once you have done your research and decided what it is you want to sell, you can go to one of the freelancer sites such as elance.com and rentacoder.com, or even fiverr.com. They have tens of thousands of freelance writers available to you. You describe what it is you want, and interested writers will bid on your proposal.

The advantages of using one of these freelance writers is that it saves you time, and time is money. You can probably find a better writer than you are, and it helps you build credibility in a niche through the availability of lots of different original publications.

The disadvantages are that it is not easy to find a good writer. You need to check the quality of the manuscript carefully once you get it; and you must check to see that the material is not plagiarized.

After posting a bid I generally get five to ten responses in a day or so, and maybe another ten during the following week. It does take a bit of time and research to study these in detail and make a good selection.

Here are some helpful hints for buying report content from freelance writers:

NEVER hire a writer from outside the United States if possible. (I will occasionally consider Canada, England, New Zealand or Australia.) You want your material written in colloquial American English, by native American-English speakers. Period. (The exscception is, of course, if you are writing for the Canadian, British, Kiwi or Aussie market!).

No matter how talented and multi-lingual a writer in India or some other third-world country might **claim** to be, or actually be, there is no substitute for a writer producing material in his or her native language. Generally your lowest bids will come from India. Don't be tempted. Forewarned is forearmed.

NEVER ask for bids on an "ebook" or "book". Always ask for bids on a "report". For psychological reasons you will always get higher bids for exactly the same product if you ask for a book rather than a report.

Look at the evaluations given by past users of a particular writer. Look at the writer's "rating". Go only for 4 or 5 "stars" out of five, or whatever the two top ratings are. (And never be the guinea pig for a first-time writer with no feedback rating whatsoever.)

Be certain to tell the potential author: your title; your outline; how fast you want it (7-14 days is reasonable depending on length); exactly how long you want it to be (see what length material others are offering on KDP and Smashwords. I generally go for fifty to a hundred 8.5 x 11 pages, and ask for a bid on fifty); and what you are willing to pay (I usually say "open" and see what bids come in.)

Once you get a price from a writer you think you like, consider saving money by bargaining the price down. This generally works. Thank them for bidding and that you feel they would be great for the job. BUT, the bid is outside your budget. "If you can lower your bid by $xxx (try 20% off the bid) I will select you immediately. Thanks." Most of the time you will get an OK. Of course, you probably can't use this idea more than once or twice with a given writer!

You will receive a huge range of bids, as much as 10X from lowest to highest. This is not necessarily a reflection of quality or anything more than how hungry a particular writer may be at the moment your request was received.

You can expect to pay between $75.00 and $450.00 for good work. Once you know your cost, now you must study the economics. Can you sell a dozen $9.97 to cover (net) the $75.00? Or seventy or so to cover $450.00?

OUTSOURCING OTHER TASKS

In general, I prefer to do things myself. Whether I am writing a book or article, creating a website, designing a book cover or whatever else, doing it myself costs zero dollars, and I have 100% control. But ego satisfaction aside, **TIME IS MONEY**. Unless you are fortunate enough to have an excess of time and no urgency whatsoever in getting a project done quickly you simply MUST outsource various "pieces" of projects.

Over the years I have used the most frequently mentioned sources of hundreds of thousands of individuals worldwide who will do almost anything for a price. These include Elance and Rent-A-Coder, among others. In using these sites you create a project and put it out for bids. You will get from five to twenty responses which you must evaluate.

The responses can run anywhere from thirty dollars to hundreds of dollars for the same "report". I always found evaluating various bids to be rather time-consuming, and I occasionally have chosen a person to do a job only to be very disappointed in the results. I spent a lot of time and a fair amount of money and accomplished little.

Then I rather recently learned about a website that is God's gift to anyone trying to make money on the internet, and especially self-publishers. The site is **fiverr.com**. If you want to spend an enjoyable afternoon go to the site and search through all of the categories. Prepare to be amazed! What individuals will do for $5.00 (of which they get a whopping $4.00) is absolutely mind-boggling! (Want someone to dance naked in the Fountain of Trevi holding your logo, you got it!)

I use Fiverr for three specific publishing tasks, all of which I can do myself for free, but five bucks saves me many hours of my time. I get better results than I used to get by paying far more money at the conventional outsourcers.

The three tasks I always outsource to Fiverr (and a fourth I sometimes do) are:

Formatting my text for Kindle, including the painful-to-create active "clickable" table of contents (TOC).

Formatting my text for Smashwords to include their all-important "Premium Catalog" in my book's distribution. This special formatting is beyond my capabilities, at least within a "five-dollars-worth" time-frame.

Formatting "back-cover/spine/front-cover" three-piece covers for Amazon's Create Space paper-back-book print-on-demand platform. If you happen to be really good with Adobe Photo Shop you can probably whip these out yourself and save five bucks. Personally, anything that comes with a half-inch thick instruction book and costs more than ten bucks hasn't a prayer of seeing my computer hard-drive!

In each of the above three cases I provide 100% of everything. The "Fiverr" person injects no creativity, just the ability to perform the special formatting needed.

The fourth? Creating the front cover. Without outsourcing I find this task enjoyable, easy and fast, as I describe elsewhere in this book. There are many at Fiverr who do great covers, but here we get into "creating" as opposed to formatting. You need to describe what it is you want and hope you can get the message across to someone whose first language is probably not English. I've gotten some great front covers for five bucks, but I've also gotten many that if nothing else were good for a laugh!

To help you choose a "Fiverr-person", Fiverr makes it very easy. Their search function, for example, "Format a Kindle book", brings up the profiles of anywhere from a handful to dozens of individuals who, for five bucks, will format your manuscript for Kindle. The profiles are excellent, and I have found to be very accurate. First of all, every comment, good and bad, that the person has ever received for their work, is shown. You can get a pretty good idea of what to expect reading through these comments.

Of some importance is the length of time the individual has been associated with Fiverr, with a special designation given to those who have successfully completed projects over a very long time

period. I pay some attention to this but it is not a deal-breaker if the person happens to be relatively new to Fiverr.

Then there is the all-important "country of origin". The general outsourcing advice is to use only people for whom English is their first language. To me this only really applies when I am seeking the outsourcer to do something creative, not simple (for them, obviously not for me) formatting of exactly what I send them. I also reason that four-bucks may be a lot of money to someone in India or some other third-world country. When I see a listing from someone in the USA I really question why in the world they would do anything for that sort of money.

Are they total losers incapable of earning real money? Are they simply out of work and anything helps? Or do they enjoy doing this stuff for practice? For fun? Ego satisfaction?

With that said, I have had excellent results with EVERY Fiverr I have ever used, irrespective of country of residence. I've used India, Croatia, Liberia, Macedonia and the USA, and many other countries, all with equally good results. I shy away from outsourcing to Pakistan, Egypt, Iraq, Iran and Saudi Arabia (and yes, there are Fiverrs there too) for hard-to-explain gut prejudices.

My advice: save time, use Fiverr. You'll thank me later!

SETTING YOUR PRICE

If you are paying $100.00 for a report that you plan to sell for $0.97 you will need to sell over a hundred copies to break even. But selling at $9.97 you only need to sell eleven to be making a profit. Ah, decisions, decisions. You will only know after a great deal of experience how to price your various offerings. Personally I sell almost everything in ebook format at the $9.97 price point. I can always adjust downwards if I am unhappy with my results. For the print-on-demand version, and my website .pdf download version, I usually add $10.00.

You cannot sell your book at a **lower** price anywhere, under the Terms & Conditions of the various publishers.

Some self-publishing authors take other pricing approaches. They will start at a low price, such as $3.97 for a few weeks, then raise the price by a dollar periodically, and keep doing this until sales decline over a given period. This is known in Economics 101 as finding the "point of diminishing returns".

There are other authors who do "Kindle Shorts" which sell for $0.99 to $2.99, hoping for high volume to obtain maximum revenue. I believe that properly packaged **any** worthy item can be sold for at least $9.97. I've never experimented with Kindle Shorts, but you may wish to experiment. **In general I believe most authors <u>under-price</u> their products. Unfortunately, because of this, ebook buyers expect to pay far less than they should for a given book.**

You might also wish to try an "odd" price, such as $9.31 which might, for some obscure psychological reason, cause someone to buy your item out of either curiosity or pity!

Have self-confidence in your products. Have the guts to believe: "This Is <u>**Worth**</u> More". "It's a bargain at <u>**twice**</u> my price!" If you are providing something of value, don't be shy, up the price.

Bear in mind, many ebooks sell thousands of copies. Alas, many do not, in fact, some do not sell any at all. What separates the winners from the losers is the research you do on your niche, and the title, the cover and the description, and your post-publishing marketing efforts. REMEMBER: It is common knowledge in the publishing industry that **covers** sell books.

Compared to the royalties book authors are accustomed to getting from publishers (around 5% is common) the commissions (i.e., royalties) authors get from Amazon KDP and other publishers are outstanding! Anything you price below $2.99 pays 35% commission. (Personally I do not sell at this level.) Anything you price between $3.00 and $9.99 the commission jumps to an amazing 70%!

The 35% royalty option is for any book you price between $0.99 and $2.98, and **over** $9.99. The 70% option is for books you price between $2.99 and $9.99. Testing by many ebook marketers have found the best price points to be $3.97, $4.97, $7.97, and

$8.97. Personally I use $9.97 for almost anything.

It is a truism that almost **anything** will sell at $2.99, the figure at which almost any viewer will click to buy if only out of curiosity. People don't think twice buying at that level. This is what most ebook buyers "expect" to pay. My ego refuses to allow me to price my precious volumes so low, even if I may be losing sales!

Amazon and Smashwords do deduct a "delivery fee" per megabyte (mb) of upload to their users' devices. While it is relatively small amount per mb, if you are selling a very long item you should look at the possibility of a higher retail price at the 35% royalty option.

I do not like the fact that there publishers can **sell** your material at any price **they** choose. Although commissions are paid to you based upon the retail price you set, you might find yourself competing with Amazon if you are selling your own ebook elsewhere at full retail price.

Here is a helpful hint that has stood the test of marketing time since the days of mail order shopping: <u>ALWAYS END YOUR SELLING PRICE WITH A "7"</u>. Your price is $3.97 not $3.99. It is $9.97 not $9.99. I have split-tested on a number of occasions and have proven to myself that this conventional wisdom is real. (It's origin is reportedly *Life Magazine's* original very successful subscription price of $7.77).

I price most items at $9.97, and receive about $6.97 commission per sale. Sell a hundred, get a check for $697.00, a thousand (not at all impossible) a check for $6,970.00! That is for ONE single item. Some ebook marketers have hundreds, some thousands, of titles for sale at the same time..

If you sell at any price $10.00 and above, the commission drops back to a still-respectable 35%. If you do the math you will see that the first higher price at 35% that brings in more commission than $9.99 at 70% is $19.99.

I have seen individual ebooks commonly offered at $49.97 and $147.00 and $197.00. I have seen many ebook courses sell for $997 and higher. I buy lots of this stuff, and so do others. I have always believed that paying for valuable information is the best investment I can make. The e-publishers are NOT set up for sales at these levels. This higher priced stuff is the land of the websites.

If you have a multi-chapter ebook you can simply chop it up and sell each chapter or set of chapters as a separate ebook! You can list it in as "one of a series". One tactic often used is to give the first book out as a freebie, to inspire purchase of the others in the series.

But here is a pricing dilemma. Most ebook independent publishers agree that the best price for **anything**, even a book easily worth fifty bucks, is $2.99. Apparently anyone who has found your item through a search won't think twice about paying three bucks.

If one can get fifteen sales out of twenty (very likely) visitors at $2.99 you make more money than selling two or three (**not** always likely) at $9.97. It is very easy, however, to split-test the same item at different prices. But as I said above, my record is stuck at $9.97!

So there you have it. This is how you create and price your masterpieces!

The most important thing is **GET STARTED**. I can make you a **100% guarantee**: if you have no books published you won't make a dime self-publishing! Proceed accordingly.

CHAPTER 4

<u>TO ISBN OR NOT TO ISBN</u>

To ISBN or not to ISBN, that is the question! Ah, Shakespeare. This is the <u>I</u>nternational <u>S</u>tandard <u>B</u>ook <u>N</u>umber system.

Now that you have written your book it is time to learn all of the miscellaneous other items and skills you will need to get it published. ISBN numbers (a common redundancy because the last "N" stands for "number") are one consideration.

Bowker Company (bowkerlink.com and myidentifiers.com) is the sole provider of ISBN numbers, the official "U. S. ISBN Agency".   Bowker maintains two web-based resources, *Books In Print* and *Global Books In Print* that permit a search by anyone for any and all books currently available anywhere on the planet.

Contrary to a popular misconception, an ISBN number does **not** convey a copyright. It is simply an identifier of the publisher that facilitates listing of a book in various data bases. Why then would anyone want one, especially in light of the fact that they are rather expensive? That is a **very** good question.

How expensive? Anywhere from $1.00 each to $125.00 each, depending on how many you buy from Bowker, who has a monoply. Talk about a quantity discount! If you buy one ISBN number you will pay $125.00 for it. Buy ten for $250.00 and you're down to $25.00 each. Buy a hundred for $575.00 and it's now $5.75 each. Want a real bargain? Buy a thousand for a thousand bucks and it's 1/125th the cost of buying one at a time. Costco beware!

Don't want to buy your own ISBN number at these exorbitant prices? Well, you don't have to! At Amazon Kindle they do not even require one, because in general an ISBN number serves no purpose for a "not physically printed" ebook. Smashwords does require an ISBN for ebooks because certain of their distribution platforms want one for indexing purposes. If you do not have your own, Smashwords supplies one for free, though you cannot use it anywhere else.

If you are selling your book from your website as a .pdf file there is no legal requirement that it have an ISBN number. It will never be listed in Bowker's data bases, but I can see no real advantage to that as far as your bottom line is concerned. Bowker would probably disagree.

So when is an ISBN number important? When you are selling books in physical print form. CreateSpace, Amazon's print-on-demand platform, offers three different ISBN options.

For **free** Amazon will assign you an ISBN number. You can't beat the price! This number is unique to this one book edition and cannot be used anywhere else. You MUST allow Amazon to assign this ISBN to your book when you apply (as you should) for "Expanded Distribution – Libraries and Academic Institutions". You cannot ever use your own ISBN for this particular distribution channel.

For all of the many other Amazon distribution channels, you can allow CreateSpace to assign the free ISBN number. When they do, the "Imprint of Record" that shows up as the "publisher" in all data bases will be "CreateSpace Independent Publishing Platform". Neither you, nor any publishing company you own or are working with, shows up as the publisher.

You can, however, for only $10.00, buy an ISBN number from CreateSpace (who buys them in bulk from Bowker) that will allow you to show whoever you want as "publisher". You cannot use this ISBN number anywhere else, and you still must allow Amazon to assign their own ISBM for "Libraries and Academic Institutions", but you do get your name in lights!

Want an ISBN number of your very own that you can use anywhere in addition to Create Space but don't want to pay Bowker $125.00? You can save $26.00 at CreateSpace who will sell you a "Custom Universal ISBN" for $99.00! (But you still need the CreateSpace assigned ISBN for "Libraries and Academic Institutions".)

What if you want to have your very own ISBN number for all of CreateSpace's platforms, but still want library distribution? You will need to open up two separate CreateSpace accounts, one exclusively for the library option using their assigned ISBN, and one for all other distribution channels using your own ISBN. CreateSpace has no mechanism within a single account for accomplishing this ISBN split.

So this gets back to: "Why do I want an ISBN number at all?". The answer is, you don't, sort of! You do not unless you become a serious publisher of multiple titles and want all of your books to show up in data bases with you or some designated company as the publisher. Will this help you sell a lot more books? Probably not. Will it help you keep your various titles and various distribution channels separate and organized within your own records? For my publisher, Lions Pride Publishing Co., LLC, that apparently is the case. For a single title they assign different ISBN numbers to Kindle, Smashwords, CreateSpace and to their website-downloadable .pdf file. That's just $4.00 per book, once they've forked over a thousand dollars to Bowker!

Let's say you decide to buy ISBNs from Bowker. You sign up for an account at myidentifiers.com or bowkerlink.com. Buy your ISBNs, and you will have an organization dashboard containing all of the numbers you bought. Click on a number, and you are taken to the first of four sections for listing your book.

The first section is "Title and Cover". Here you list your book title and subtitle, and enter a 350 word or less book description. I simply use the description I created for the back cover of my Amazon CreateSpace paperback print-on-demand book. Just cut and paste. I may be allowed more words, but I just can't be bothered writing a larger description just for Bowker. Next you upload the .jpg image of your **front** cover. Lastly you upload your book text, as described below.

There are two things you **must** remember to do at this point. One is to take your "basic" Microsoft Word book copy which contains no ISBN numbers or other identifier (i.e., Kindle, Smashwords, CreateSpace, website) and add the information that relates to the specific ISBN number you are in the process of identifying. It is incredibly easy to screw this up unless you are very organized. Remember, you are dealing with four separate "editions" of your book: Kindle, Smashwords, CreateSpace, and your website .pdf. All are identical wording except for the title page which identifies the ISBN and the publishing platform.

Once you have created the correct "edition", convert this specific Word .docx document into a .pdf file (portable document format). If you have Microsoft Word 2010 or later this is a simple direct- conversion function from a drop-down menu. If not, Google ".doc to .pdf converter" and you can download a conversion program for free. Convert, and upload this .pdf to your dashboard at

Bowker. Next go to the second of four functions, "Contributors".

Here you list the author, and upload the author's bio, cut and pasted from the rear book cover. You are allowed 350 words and if you want to embellish it to fit that is fine, but I consider it a waste of time. Nothing else is needed in this section. In fact, throughout the entire process, ONLY take the time to put information in places Bowker spots with an apteryx "*" symbol. Go to section three, "Format and Size".

Enter the medium specific to this ISBN, either "Print" or "eBook".

If print, click "Paperback" in the dropdown menu. If you chose ebook, "electronic" automatically populates. **Ignore** all of the other stuff on the page, and drop down to your primary and secondary subject, which you must choose from a drop-down menu. Of course nothing in that menu will actually **match** your book, so you just have to get as close as possible! Go directly to the last section, "Sales and Pricing".

Here you choose "United States" and "On Demand" from dropdown menus. Then enter your date of publication (I use the date I'm in their website). There is one school of thought that says NEVER enter a publication date so that years from now your book seems "fresh".

Next enter your target audience from a dropdown menu. Here again you will be entering a rough approximation of reality! Then drop down and enter your pricing.

As discussed above, I always end my price with a "7" because conventional wisdom says it actually makes a difference! For Kindle, Smashwords and CreateSpace be certain you have chosen your price to maximize your royalties as discussed elsewhere in this book. Enter "US Dollars" for currency. You do not have to complete anything else. Just go to the bottom right and hit "Submit". If you have failed to enter everything needed a pop up will tell you what you need to add.

Once you have this completed you will see a symbol on your dashboard next to the ISBN that indicates "Processing Information". Within a few days this changes to a green check. Your book is then in the official ISBN system as yours and yours alone!

To summarize, at least when you are first starting out, especially if you are not flush with start-up cash, just forget about buying ISBN numbers. The process described above is exactly as complicated (although it shouldn't take more than twenty minutes) as any of the publishing platforms, it just adds an extra publishing step that can be avoided.

One other minor annoyance happens occasionally. You may get an email from Amazon or Smashwords indicating that your ISBN is invalid. This simply means that Bowker has not completed their approval process, which can take a few days. I just ignore the email because they automatically continue approving your book for publication once Bowker clears the ISBN. This minor annoyance does not occur if you use the

ISBNs available on the publishing platforms themselves as described above.

Later on, when your publishing cash flow begins, you can decide whether it makes sense to purchase ISBN numbers in bulk from Bowker to show you or your publisher listed officially in data bases, and to facilitate your own record keeping.

CHAPTER 5

<u>YOUR TITLE IS THE KEY</u>

Unless you are writing fiction, you will be selling "INFORMATION" to individuals who are looking for "How To...." reports and books on almost anything you can imagine. They search for the information on Amazon or Google by entering their needs in a search function. <u>Your job is to learn what people are searching for, produce a product that fulfills their need at a price they will pay, and then seeing to it that your product shows up prominently in a search result.</u>

Why do people buy information? Primarily because they are either too busy or too lazy to find it for themselves. They are willing to pay a nominal sum for the instant gratification of pressing a button and finding what they want effortlessly and without wading through pages of fluff. And many individuals like you and me can get rich guiding them as to which button to press!

Beyond information-oriented written books and reports, people also buy all sorts of fiction, (especially romance novelettes), children's books, poetry, science fiction, and just about anything else you can imagine. You will need to decide whether you prefer to offer non-fiction or fiction works. Personally, I provide a mix of both. And both can be wildly profitable.

It has been proven time and time again that people **buy the TITLE**. This is a critical piece of information to know. There are documented cases of books that hardly sold at all until the author changed just the title and it became a best seller! In fact, if I have an item listed in Kindle or Smashwords that isn't selling well I simply change the title. It often changes my results to multiple sales!

I recall a classic example of this from a few decades back. There was a business book titled something like: "How To Start a Business". It did not sell a single copy. Then the author changed the title to a long acronym: "WNGFANPSIANB" and it became a best seller! It stood for: "**W**hy **N**ice **G**uys **F**ail **A**nd **N**asty **P**eople **S**ucceed **I**n **A** **N**ew

Business". I offer this from memory, and it is probably a bit off, but you get the idea.

In Amazon Kindle you are allowed a Title but not a SubTitle. My preference is: "How To (keyword/keyword/keyword)". Followed by (as an added part of my title substituting for a sub-title): "x# Tips To (keyword/keyword/keyword)". The "x#" should always be an odd number such as 3, 5, 7, 9, 11 etc. Split testing has proven time and again that odd numbers in a title increase sales for whatever deep psychological reason. Don't ask me.

It is a very good idea to do a thorough keyword search, and see how many keywords you can work into your title. It is also a good idea once you decide on a title to try to register a domain name as close to your title as possible.

Paying attention to a properly crafted title can be the difference between self-publishing success and failure. A killer cover and a great title has sold many a mediocre book!

CHAPTER 6

<u>YOUR DEDICATION – BROWNIE POINTS?</u>

I doubt whether a dedication has ever helped sell a book, but I suspect it could hurt if done poorly.

In every book publishing platform you will be allowing a potential buyer to download some percentage of the beginning of your book. Anywhere from ten to twenty-five percent is common. You want the potential buyer to see just enough of your writing to whet their appetite to buy the book. They will **always** see the dedication.

Want to impress the heck out of a girlfriend? Hand her a physical copy of the book you just published! Guaranteed to impress! A nice added touch is to write a greeting inside the front cover, signed using your full author-name, and then "Love, (you)". For even more brownie points you could have include in the dedication: "To my beautiful and wonderful girlfriend (name) who gives light to my life and wings to my pen". Or whatever. Of course, unless by coincidence your next love has the same name this only works once! Anyway, you get the picture.

Forgive my obvious chauvinism. I'm certain the above works just as well for a female author to her boyfriend, or any other combination of affections as fits your personal situation. Dedications work well for wives and husbands too!

Dedicating your book to Jesus, you childhood teddy-bear, or your pet tarantula probably isn't a great idea!

In general the dedication should be short, one or two sentences, centered in the middle of the page.

One exception, favoring a longer dedication, is if you have been helped along the way by some **famous** person or persons. Including those persons in your dedication could add credibility to you personally, especially in a "how to" book.

Don't waste a lot of time agonizing over a dedication. Many books have none at all. Just make it short and sweet and move on to more important things.

CHAPTER 7

<u>YOUR IMPORTANT TABLE OF CONTENTS</u>

<u>Your Table of Contents is more important than you might imagine.</u> As mentioned above, your potential buyer will certainly see this in the "read x% for free" offer you stipulate. The point here is **make your chapter titles interesting.** The potential buyer should see these and say to themselves: "Wow, I need to read about that!". "And that!". "And surely **that**!". It can be the difference between a sale and a pass. You want sales. You hate passes.

With that said, try to keep your chapter headings short enough that they all occupy a single line. It simply makes for a cleaner-looking table of contents.

As a general rule, books with a lot of relatively short chapters sell better than books of the same word-count with fewer longer chapters. This is especially true with non-fiction books which are easier to "break up" into smaller chapters. In fiction books, there has been a trend recently for major best-selling authors to offer as many as fifty or more short chapters!

Your Table of Contents (often referred to as the TOC) should at most take up two pages. A single page is better, though that limits you to under thirty chapters or so.

Always call your chapters "Chapter", not "Part" or "Section" or "Item" or anything else. The reason for this is that certain ebook platforms key in on the word "Chapter" and cannot otherwise properly format your book.

Double space, make it easy to read, and if you have a few items carry over to a second page. If necessary consider cutting down font size from 16 point to 14 point or even as small as 12 point.

In self-published ebooks and print-on-demand books there are **NO** page numbers! That is true throughout the book, and thus true for the Table of Contents. You have no choice here. This is simply how it works with these publishing platforms. The only time you might want to use page numbers is on the .pdf file pages and TOC that customers will be downloading when they purchase directly from your website.

And for ebook readers it is important that your TOC be "clickable"`. The reader expects to be able to click on a Chapter heading and be taken directly to the start of that chapter anywhere within your book. This requires special file formatting which will be discussed later in this book.

Your Table of Contents is an important part of your book. Give it the attention it deserves and you will be rewarded with many more sales over time.

CHAPTER 8

<u>CRITICAL PROFIT POWER WORDS</u>

It is very important to **properly**, through the use of time-tested and proven "power-words, write the description of your book, and the information about yourself as the author.

These descriptions will appear on the back cover of your book, and will be read prior to a buyer making that all-important decision to click "BUY". They will also appear in all of the critical data bases, from Bowker's ISBN registry to Amazon, Barnes and Noble, Smashwords and everywhere else your book will be sold.

My suggestion is that you write these book and author descriptions without giving any thought in advance to including "power words" in the descriptions. After doing so, then refer to the power-words lists that follow below. These are words that can be substituted for words you have chosen to use yourself. Once you get the hang of the substitution process it becomes quite easy and takes little time, and markedly improves your copy.

Over time, and with experience, you will learn to write your descriptions without the need for referring to the lists.

The lists that follow have been proven over decades of study by language-response experts to be words to which buyers react favorably. I didn't just make these up. They are compiled from the best information I have found published over many years.

Do not overdo their use. Using seven to ten throughout your book description and a few in your personal biography will go a very long way towards increasing sales. Using too many might make the text too obviously sales oriented or stilted. I have tried split-testing on two parallel websites, one with a crappy description with zero power words and the other substituting suitable power-words. I was quite impressed with the difference in results. If you have the time and inclination I suggest you try this split test to see just how important the proper use of power words can be.

Here are power words you should consider using:

WORDS AT OR NEAR THE BEGINNING:

Announcing; emerging; introducing; how to; just arrived; sure fire; launching; it's here; the truth about; unlock; at last; discover; uncover; secrets of ...; Breaking News!; Stop!; Listen!.

POWER WORDS ABOUT YOU, THE AUTHOR:

Noted; famous; professional; successful; insider; expert; skill; perspective; honored; gifted.

POWER WORDS TO EXPLAIN "WHY IT'S GOOD":

Timely; easy; helpful; powerful; instructive; quick; amazing; exciting; wonderful; sensational; popular; miracle; edge; simple; simplified; excellent; revolutionary; informative; reliable; promising.

POWER WORDS RELATED TO SIZE:

Unlimited; mammoth; huge; big; colossal; gigantic; sizeable; full; crammed; liberal; largest; enormous; tremendous; commanding; compact; generous; immense.

POWER WORDS RELATED TO PRICE/VALUE:

Bargain; bonanza; reward; underpriced; reduced; affordable; refundable; growth; portfolio; fortune; discount; lowest; value; bottom line; wealth; profitable; save; profit; no-risk; zero-risk;

POWER WORDS RELATED TO "WHY IT'S BETTER":

Improved; pioneering; technology; beautiful; genuine; simplistic; security; quality; imagination; high tech; strong; important; practical; special; luxury; new; authentic; tested; better; innovative; terrific; unsurpassed; greatest; latest; ultimate; magic; sturdy; superior; fascinating; astonishing; complete; outstanding; personalized.

POWER WORDS THAT ARE BUYING "HOOKS";

Breakthrough; confidential; unusual; revealing; monumental; unparalleled; surprise; zinger; approved; endorsed; exclusive; blockbuster; astonishing; awesome; dazzling; electrifying; fantastic; incredible; phenomenal; unique.

POWER WORDS THAT CAN HELP CLOSE A SALE:

Limited; immediately; now; sale; guaranteed; urgent; last chance; scarce; quickly; last minute; special offer; unconditional; hurry; limited offer; time-sensitive.

MISCELLANEOUS POWER WORDS FOR ANY SITUATION:

YOU; spotlight; wanted; interesting; highest; will power; colorful; lifetime; focus; gift; survival; fundamentals; suddenly; absolutely; shrewd; challenge; engaging; charming; cheerful; enhanced; expanded; compose; easily; attractive; competitive; delighted; compromise; mainstream;

selected; storage; download; odd; opportunities; obsession; Information City; surging; lavishly; sampler; weird; durable; dynamic; educational; alert; delivered; soar; direct; revisited; destiny; love; exploit; direct; accelerate; adorable; advance; boost; captivating; clear; complete; compelling; comprehensive; cool; crazy; critical; effective; effortless; first; initial; powerful; revealing; easy; explosive; extreme; eye popping; famous; fast; friendly; gracious; gripping; crucial; current; dominant; hair raising; handy; helpful; heavy duty; high impact; high powered; high tech; amplify; amusing; appealing; hot; ignite; important; in depth; super; unlock; uncover; ….exposed; ….revealed; ….explained; beware.

MY TEN FAVORITE POWER WORDS : Free; unique; secrets; useful; valuable; rare; proven; daring; startling; remarkable.

Many of the above power words could be classified in more than one category, but I've tried to put them in logical groups with little duplication. I purposely chose not to alphabetize them because I think it better inspires one to read through each list. Personally, when I see an alphabetized list I tend to stop reading at around "D"!

There are no hard and fast rules regarding how many of these power words should be used in any given description, item of text, sales letter or press release. One could probably write an entire paragraph using nothing **but** these words, with an occasional "a". "and" and "the" thrown in! But the final copy must flow naturally, as if you were excited about something and were describing it to a friend. There is a fine line between "cheesy" and "classy" copy. Try having friends and family read different versions of your descriptions and see if you can get a consensus on which wording gets the most juices flowing.

Generally speaking, I go with my gut. If I read some copy I wrote, and can honestly say to myself: "That's pretty darn convincing. I'd probably buy that.", then I'm pretty confident that in general my prospective buyers will be enticed to press the magic "BUY IT NOW" button!

CHAPTER 9

<u>WRITING YOUR IMPORTANT DESCRIPTION</u>

Equally important to the title and cover is your book description. This is what can close the sale after your title and cover art have attracted your potential buyer's initial interest.

Use as many words or characters as the publishing platform allows. Look at your keyword research. It is central to your Description. Look at possible "power words".

You must pick a "Category". I always try to select mine based on the best-selling books in my niche. This takes a bit of searching through the publishing sites. You will end up clicking through something like: store>books>nonfiction>(your general niche)>(your sub-niche)>(your refined sub-sub-niche).

In writing the Description use keywords that are highly relevant to your book content, not necessarily those with high search volume. Just study your basic keyword research (see Chapter 11) and write your description accordingly.

You might ask a question to which you know that the answer is "YES". "Do you want to get rid of acne? If you do, than this is the book for YOU. In (your title) you will not only learn (find popular questions through "yahooanswers.com") but you will also learn (see again the Yahoo! answers) to help you." **YOU, YOU, YOU,** used as often as space allows, addressing everything you learned for which readers in your niche are searching.

At the end if I have space I'll often add: <u>"You deserve the best and it gets no better than (my title). Buy it NOW."</u>

Always try to work in some extra enhancements: I frequently use "Limited Edition"; "Collector's Edition"; "RED HOT"; "The NEW BEST SELLER"; "LIMITED

DISCOUNT EDITION", whatever you can think of. Be certain to add a "call to action" such as: "BUY NOW".

You can add a link here that is not overt selling. You could try: "Visit my website at (yoursite.com) and get a free title of equal value" (or a free report or whatever freebie you can imagine). This can be a money-maker even if someone doesn't buy your book, because you can collect their email address for future marketing!

CHAPTER 10

ABOUT YOU

THE TOPIC-EXPERT AUTHOR

There are two basic forms of the "About the Author" text you will be creating. There is the abbreviated version that will show up on every book search, and on the back cover of your book. Then there is the longer version inserted towards the end of your book.

Both are usually written in third person. Someone other than you is supposedly writing it. It is important to refer to the "Power Words" in Chapter 8 and to get as many of these words as possible into the text, along with a few searchable key-words and phrases.

There is only **one** major purpose for this self-aggrandizing biographic text. **You need to convince your potential buyer that you have the knowledge and the expertise to be writing the book in the first place!** Otherwise, why should they trust your information? This is a lot easier for a non-fiction book than, say, a romance novel. In the latter case the best I could come up with would be a sob story about my own life that would relate in some way to the key character in my fiction book.

For a non-fiction work, your **direct experience** in the genre, your **relevant education**, and your **years studying the topic** are all critical to explain. You must have your horn tooted, but it must not sound like a load of fluffy bull-crap. <u>This appears in the lead paragraph of your "About The Author" section.</u> It is all the potential buyer cares about. **"Why should I listen to this person?"** You **MUST** answer that question well, and early.

The fact that you were born in a ghetto and have pulled you and your family out of a rat hole through your writing expertise might make interesting reading, but it won't go too far to help sell your book. If your lifetime hobby relates to the material in the book, that's worthy of note. But if you are writing a book on rose care and happen to be a two-handicapper skip mentioning that up front. I'm sure you get the picture!

Putting a "homey" touch at the end cannot hurt. Having a loving family, a wife of forty years, four kids, seven grandkids and a great-grand kid on the way provides a certain "Awww" factor. So does having two exceptionally cute dogs and a cuddly fat cat. It shows you're more or less human.

Stating that you are donating some or all of your profits to some familiar and worthy cause cannot hurt either. Just be certain that you follow through on the promise when you make the sales.

The length of this text, as far as this book "chapter" is concerned, should be at least two pages. If your book is short, say forty pages, you do not want five of them to be all about you!

This is, in a sense, your resume'. You are applying for a job, that of author, and your "potential boss" is your buyer. A proper job-resume' summarizes your **achievements** as they relate to the job for which you are applying. Your date of birth, place of birth, and astrological sign and interests are **totally** unimportant. The only time I might suggest you allude to your age is when it is exceptional for the topic in hand. A sex manual by a 93 year old might raise eyebrows. If written by a 13 year old the same eyebrows might raise but for a completely different reason!

Treat the "About Author" text as being very important to your success. The potential buyer must "buy" that you have something to say he or she wants to hear and is willing to pay to hear it. If you come across as anything other than the "resident expert" you diminish your chance of making the sale. A little puffery here goes a long way.

Happy puffing!

CHAPTER 11

<u>KEYWORDS AND TAGS</u>

The fundamental effort to making self-publishing marketing work is **<u>KEYWORD RESEARCH.</u>** You have to be ready and willing to spend a great deal of time at the outset before you can think about posting content to your publishing platforms. Personally I find this research to be fun and interesting. If you look at it that way, and not as a "chore", you will greatly increase your chances for big-time success.

KEYWORD RESEARCH is the single most important aspect of marketing self-published books. You actually have two basic choices to consider. You can focus on a very broad-based market with a large number of searches. This may intuitively seem like the best way to go, and many go that way. But most self-published internet infopreneur-writers, myself included, look for specialized "niche" markets, highly focused, but with far fewer searches.

Here is where internet marketing experience comes into play. I look for 15,000 to 40,000 "collective" monthly searches for a topic. Fewer is too limiting, more is too broad a market. This figure may not be optimum in other internet marketing efforts, but it seems to hold true for self-published books.

By "collective" search numbers I mean the total combined searches for any wording that you can imagine that shows that someone is looking for the exact same highly-focused niche product. For example, if you are writing on "hunting deer with a crossbow", searches for "deer hunting with a crossbow", "hunting deer with a crossbow", "crossbow deer hunting", and "deer crossbow hunting" would all be added together for the "collective" monthly search figure.

When your buyer is searching for an ebook or print-on-demand book to buy, the following are the sorts of terms with which they will lead their query:

I need help with (training my emu); (fixing my garage door); (my pistol aim);

How do you (fix a leaky faucet?) (make a Doberman obey?) (find a hot date?);

How can I cure (my slice?) (a bad case of acne?) (my husband's snoring?).;

What can I do to (lose weight?) (find cheap airline seats?); (find a wife?).

In addition to these four, seven other common "lead-ins" are:

"How to stop....?"; "Help me to...."; Help with....": "Get help with...."; "Where can I ....?"; "How should I ....?"; "How would I ....?".

Use these eleven lead-in phrases in your keyword search. Obviously there are infinite possibilities, but I find sticking to just these eleven helps me stay sane!

There are five basic ways to make money with self-publishing:

Sell original your books and reports as ebooks or print-on-demand;

Sell your one-book publishing platform as you would sell a developed website;

Build up your publishing site with a number of different items on your bookshelf. If you can document decent earnings, you can sell the entire site including the valuable 100% rights to all of the books. I have heard of such sales in the $50,000 and up range!

You could offer your services to others helping them create covers, great titles, and great descriptions.

Use your books to drive traffic to market your own products on your own website.

GOOGLE RESEARCH

Let's look at what Google has to offer us. Go to any Google page with a Google search function, and enter your keyword. When the search list appears, go to the long list on the left side and click on "Related Searches". At the top of the search results will appear a list of very useful related terms. Clicking on one of these will show you the sites that are rich in those particular keywords.

Google has an excellent keyword tool.   It also has a valuable contextual (keywords appearing within the text of a book or report) targeting tool for you to use to analyze your competition. Both tools are within the "Google AdWords" program.

For starters, open up a free AdWords account, which you must have to access this useful tool. Go to adwords.google.com (You will need a website address [an actual developed site is unnecessary, just a domain name] to complete the initial sign-up form.) Register one at godaddy.com or wherever.

Next you "Create Google Account" where you will give your name and email address and make up a password. Next step will be choosing a time zone and currency in which you want to be paid. You will then be sent an email.

The email gives you an account number (copy and keep it, though I've never needed it for anything) and a special link. Click on the link, and you have confirmed your account. You then go back to the home page and sign in with your email address and the password you created.

Incidentally, if you have any other Google account, such as gmail, you can sign in to AdWords with your sign-in info for that account.

This site has an immense amount of helpful information on it. You would be well advised to spend an entire day clicking on every tab and watching every training video.

To access the keyword tool itself click on the "Reporting & Tools" tab, and on the drop-down menu click on "Keyword Tool". Then by entering your keywords and phrases, and choosing the general category from a menu, you will get a huge list showing the searches made for many terms in your niche. By checking a small box you can narrow the list down to searches more closely focused to your term. It is a good idea to do both.

To access the contextual targeting tool, click on the "Opportunities" tab, enter a few words that describe your offer, and the tool will create a series of "ad groups". When you click on the "Expand" button you see updated lists of relevant keywords. This is all incredibly helpful, and it's FREE!

BEYOND GOOGLE RESEARCH

A rather useful site which provides a somewhat different set of data than Google when you search with your keywords is: quintura.com.   (Ignore the occasional result in Russian!) Enter your search term in the box provided and click on the almost-invisible arrow on the right side of the box. You will find the URL results to be quite specific to your search terms.

Now check out alexa.com.   According to their website: "Find And Evaluate Businesses Worldwide With Alexa's Free

Web Analytics". This may well be the most useful web site out there. It is widely reported that it is the **only** site that has a truly unbiased website ranking system. It is owned by Amazon.   It ranks websites purely on search volume. I strongly suggest you study what this site has to offer. They only provide statistics for popular websites, but if you want every imaginable analytic about one of their listed sites you can find it at Alexa.

Studying details of successful sites can offer you guidance in creating your own marketing campaigns. You can also learn up to the minute "hot topics", "hot products" and "hot web pages" at no cost. Check out: answers.yahoo.com or yahooanswers.com, put in a keyword, and you will have a wealth of data on exactly what people are looking for. You must be clear on exactly who your audience is before creating material for publication. Picture your audience actually reading your book or report. Connect with them. You must be very clear on the identity of your audience.

It is absolutely essential that you spend as much time as you can studying these analyses sites and what they have to offer. In fact, from a time-spent perspective, you will find that keyword search will occupy at least half of a working day. I find these tasks to be fun, because I know they are the key to the money I make self-publishing my books.

There are MANY free keywords tools. A Google search will reveal them all. They have limitations, but there is no harm in playing around with a few to see what you can come up with.

If you want to buy a more sophisticated tool that gives you far more keyword choices and other valuable tools go to: wordtracker.com. They have a free seven-day trial so you can decide whether it is worth its price of a bit over a dollar a day.

For years I have used a tool by Brad Callen available at keywordelite.com which sells for under a hundred bucks, and is well worth it.

Never lose sight of your primary goal in working with Kindle Direct Publishing and Smashwords: **TO FIND OUT WHAT INFORMATION PEOPLE WANT TO BUY AND THEN CREATING AND SELLING IT TO THEM ON THEIR EBOOK READER!**

CHAPTER 12

FIRST IMPRESSION

THE KILLER COVER

When writing anything the idea is to **STAND OUT** from the competition. You do this with not only a killer title, but also with a killer **COVER.** This cover image is first seen as a tiny rectangle next to your description, then in a larger version once a reader clicks on it.

The cover is your "For Sale" sign. It's the first thing that catches the visitor's eye. If you check out the Amazon Kindle website and click on some Kindle covers you will see how the larger image of the cover magically appears. You must admit that some of the covers sparked your interest. You can also see how some are absolutely terrible.

Your cover MUST tell the reader what your book is all about.

There is no question that you **can** judge a book by its cover! In fact, your cover is far more important than the text of your book. I have seen mediocre books with great covers sell well. I've also seen great literary works totally flop because the cover was awful. Both of these offerings were mine!

Now "great" and "awful" are subjective terms. Beauty is in the eyes of the beholder. But this is not a beauty contest. If you want your book to have a shot at selling, your cover **MUST** contain the following elements:

BACKGROUND IMAGE

You must choose an image that immediately tells the prospective buyer: <u>"This is what you'll find inside!"</u>. This is somewhat easier to do with a non-fiction title. But even with various fiction genres, such as a romance novel, you can have a cover showing a closely-related theme, such as a generalized romantic setting. Your image, **before** you add any text on the cover whatsoever, must convey whatever your book is all about, and do it at a quick glance.

You also must be aware that no matter how beautiful your cover is in living color, most buyers will see it in living black and white on their ebook readers. (Kindle's new Flame is an exception at this writing.) Some of the best looking covers I have created in color look absolutely dreadful in black and white.

You need to choose your image with forethought. You need a logical "clear" space in the background image to add your title, subtitle, and any other text, so that it does not interfere with the message of the image.

TITLE

OK, so we discussed creating a great title in Chapter 5. This is the time to show it off! The key here is that it be readable in a **thumbnail-size image**. That means it has to be **HUGE** in the book's full sized printed version. Depending on the length of the title it can be one, two, or even three lines. The font color, from black through white and all colors in between, will depend to a large extent on the background image you selected.

The easiest to read font is Arial, dark-enhanced. Never lose sight of the fact that it must be clearly readable in a thumbnail- size image. Use ALL CAPITALS. If the background image is dark, use white lettering.

SUBTITLE

If you have a subtitle, and you should, print it centered below the title, in one or two font sizes smaller. USE ALL CAPITALS.

ADDITIONAL LOWER TEXT

Some titles lend themselves to an additional sub-sub-title located somewhere towards the bottom. See the cover of this book for an example of what I mean. USE ALL CAPITALS.

AUTHOR

At the bottom, and usually right-justified, in the smallest size font on the cover, goes: "By (Your Name)". If you happen to be a famous or even well-known best-selling author then the size of the font for your name can almost equal the size of the font used for the title! In this case your name sells the book, and little else matters. Don't put your name in a large font to satisfy your ego!

The question is, how do I actually **create** a front cover? My answer is: **"Do it yourself!".** Now I am the furthest person alive from being a graphic artist. Ask me to draw a person and it's the same two circles and four sticks that I could have done in kindergarten, only probably not as good!

There are hundreds of programs out there that you can use, from the incredibly complicated and expensive Adobe PhotoShop to the easy to use and FREE Microsoft Paint. The latter is 100% fabulous for creating covers. PhotoShop is out of my league.

Now why do I not suggest that you outsource your cover? There are any number of eager graphic artists at elance.com and rentacoder.com and fiverr.com that will be pleased to bid on your job (or in the case of Fiverr, do it for five bucks!). For starters, it's just too easy to do yourself. I can create a very decent front cover from scratch in at the most ten minutes. For me to outsource front covers I need to convey my vision of what the cover should be, put it out for bids, choose my graphic artist, and then pray my written intentions don't get lost in the translation. They usually do.

For starters, the vast majority of outsourcers use stock images. One can find literally millions of these on line. Many are free. Most of these are far from good. And you cannot be 100% certain that the image used by your outsourcer is free of copyright unless you secure the image yourself and send it to the outsourcer. Because finding and downloading the image is the most time-consuming part of creating a front cover in the first place, if you decide to do so you might just as well finish the job yourself on Microsoft Paint at zero cost.

Familiarize yourself with Microsoft Paint, which probably came with your computer. If it did not, it is a free download. It is very simple for even a zero-talent graphic artist such as me!

Load your chosen image into Paint. Resize it so you can see the whole cover on your screen. The resize function is intuitive.

At this point it is important that your image be scaled to the size book you plan to create. I do everything in 6" x 9" because I find it to be the most sellable format. So my image must have a 6:9 width to height ratio, created by adjusting either of the default "100" settings in MS Paint. Resize>60/90>disable aspect ratio, hit OK. (Be sure to disable "Maintain Aspect Ratio" or you will end up right where you started.)

It is also important that the pixel length along the long side be as required by the ebook publishing platforms. This is the time to do that as well. Resize>Pixels>disable aspect ratio.

Enter a desired figure in the long side and hit OK. The short side pixels will adjust accordingly. Some images will distort too much during this process and you may need to find another image.

Next simply click on the "A" on the taskbar, and on your image drag around to create the box within which your text will appear. If you know how to use Microsoft Word, you will see the same taskbar in Paint.

Once you type in your title text you can move it around to center it however you want. Repeat the process with all of your other text.

Where do I find my images? After much trial and error I only use fotolia.com. They have hundreds of thousands of images, all categorized with a simple search function. The most time-consuming part of front cover creation is searching for a suitable image. By the time I have viewed a few hundred I always find one I can use. The cover image on this book is from Fotolia; the text I did in MS Paint. It took me less than ten minutes to create this cover. Expect to pay Fotolia $5.00 for a "medium size" image. Download to your computer, upload to Paint, go to work finishing the cover.

This is not to say you could not spend the time to find a suitable cover image through a Google search. I just have found that straying away from Fotolia wastes my time.

Now up to here I have been talking about **FRONT** covers. This is all you need for your ebook publications. But if you decide to use Amazon's CreateSpace print-on-demand program, and you must, you will need a front **AND** back cover, and a spine, and they must be created to very exacting standards. Here, and only here, is where I outsource.

Don't get me wrong. I still create the front cover. I also create the text for the rear cover AND the text for spine of the book. It is in assembling these three elements as required that I consider five bucks to be a huge bargain! If you are very good with Adobe PhotoShop you can probably figure out how to do this for yourself in a few minutes. Personally, any program that costs more than ten bucks and comes with a half-inch thick instruction book never makes it on to my hard drive!

Google the term exactly as follows: "Bleeds (an excerpt)", download the resulting .pdf file, and print it out. It's free. (This is part of a larger publication: *CS Digital: A Practical Guide to OS Digital Possibilities".*) This is the **only** good guide I have found explaining how to create three-piece back-spine-front covers for CreateSpace. If you can follow this guide, and can use a graphics program, I'm sure you can do the cover assembly yourself. I choose to use fiver.com. For $5.00 there are any number of graphic artists who can take the front-cover/spine/back- cover you created and turn it into a single file that meets CreateSpace's requirements. I always upload the fiverr-folk them a copy of "Bleeds" so I'm certain they do it correctly.

There is a certain recommended formula for the back cover. There are essentially seven elements: Upper left corner; upper right corner; about the author; about the book; testimonials; lower left corner; and lower right corner.

If you can access a copy of the entire cover of this book on Amazon.com do so and follow that format. (Of course if you bought a printed book-on-demand copy of this book the back cover is a bit easier to access…just flip it over!)

UPPER LEFT CORNER

In a small rectangle put two lines of text which tells the search route by which someone would find your book on Amazon. This could be: non-fiction/business>real estate, or whatever matches your book.

UPPER RIGHT CORNER

A short, two line "teaser" about the book, ten to a dozen words at most, as an uncompleted sentence followed by …….

ABOUT THE AUTHOR

Across the cover write a seven to eight line blurb, which can be the same as you created for uploading to your ebook platforms. Be certain that you include a few "power words" from Chapter 8. Put the underlined black-letters heading above it:

"About The Author". Use 12 point Arial Black-Enhanced font.

ABOUT THE BOOK

Across the cover write a keyword-rich power-word-rich description of the book. Here again, you may wish to use the description you already created for the ebook platforms. This can be ten to a dozen lines. As a heading for this section use the title of your book. Use 12 point Arial Black-Enhanced font. On the line above the description I put the book title in white letters against a red background.

TESTIMONIALS

Below the book description, under the heading "Testimonials", place two very short one line testimonials. At this point in time it should be from the friends and family to whom you already sent preliminary text files for comment and can document their comments if challenged to do so.

LOWER LEFT CORNER

If you have one, (or if not just use your initials), this is where you put your logo. If you need a graphic artist to create a logo, I strongly suggest fiverr.com. There are many "Fiverrs" that do excellent logos for $5.00. This would be the same logo you would use on your book's website.

LOWER RIGHT CORNER

This is reserved for your bar code. You can create one yourself with barcode software you can buy over the internet. But why bother? Amazon CreateSpace designs one for you, and doesn't charge a dime! Let Amazon do it. Free is good. Just leave them a sufficient blank corner space.

Last but not least is the book's spine. If your book is not 1/3rd inch or wider leave the spine blank. Otherwise your logo and your book title go horizontally across the spine. You'll know the spine width after you convert to 6"x9" in Word, hit "File>Save" to learn the page quantity, and then plug the number of pages into a formula provided by CreateSpace.

This formula varies based upon the type of paper you choose to have Amazon use to print your book. You will need to give this width figure to the Fiverr-person to incorporate in the format of the back/spine/front composite cover.

When you read *"Bleeds (an excerpt)"* you will find that in creating the back-spine-front cover the **total** cover width needs to be a touch greater than twice the cover's individual front or back cover width plus the spine width. This is because Amazon needs to trim a bit all around the cover during their printing process. The same is true for the height. All of this is explained in detail in "Bleeds".

Also, when writing the text copy for your back cover, you must be certain to leave ample space around all edges for the final Amazon trimming.

This is also worth remembering when you put any text on your front cover in MS Paint: If you bring the text too close to an edge it will get sliced off. You don't want that.

If you have a relatively short title you might try arranging it on the spine one word above the other so that it can be read when on a shelf without cocking one's head to the right or left. Very few authors do this, and I think it is a big plus. This technique was taught to me by my writing mentor Dan Poynter.

To this point we a have been talking about covers for Amazon Kindle, Create Space, and Smashwords. But what about covers displayed on your websites? Personally, I'm a bit lazy here and simply use the same two-dimensional (2D) front cover I created for the three basic publishing platforms. Some authors, however, prefer the book be shown in "3D" on their websites, as if it were a physical book looked at other-than directly front-on. To create this effect there are dozens of software programs available for very little cost, some even free. Just do a Google search for "3D cover creator". You simply download the program, plug in your 2D front cover and spine, press a button, and as if by magic you have a 3D cover! If you do not want to do this yourself, by all means go to fiverr.com and for $5.00 you can find any number of folks to do it for you.

I will occasionally show the full 2D back-spine-front composite cover on my website, if I am particularly fond of the back cover text and feel that it adds value to my website.

Creating a cover may seem like a lot of work when it is described step by step as I have tried to do above. Believe me, you can create a front cover in ten minutes or less, and the text copy for the back cover and spine in five minutes if you use the "author" and "book" descriptive texts previously created for your ebook platforms.

COVERS SELL BOOKS! Keeping this reality in mind during every phase of your cover creation. You will be rewarded with increased sales. If you don't believe this, split test with a crappy cover and a great cover. See which one sells better. Prepare to be amazed!

CHAPTER 13

<u>UGLY BUT NECESSARY</u>

<u>"SMALL PRINT"</u>

The very first page that your potential buyer sees when he samples your book is this important page. It contains a number of key elements:

The book title;

The book sub-title;

The author;

The edition identity;

The ISBN number;

The copyright publisher and year;

The "Rights" paragraph;

The "small print" legal disclaimer.

Incidentally, always spell out "copyright". The use of the "c-in-a-circle" created by holding down the "ctrl" and "alt" keys while typing "c" does not reproduce well in formatting for electronic publishing.

Refer to the first page of **this** book. The Rights and Disclaimer I use are pretty similar to those used throughout the internet commerce industry. You can adjust the wording to fit your particular book, but essentially you should have all of this material in the book.

Feel free to copy my version exactly. You should, however, have your own attorney approve whatever text you plan to use, because this is the unfortunately-necessary CYA legal copy.

It is extremely important for you to include this page. It offers you a certain level of protection from plagiarism, and to some extent it reduces the possibility of financial liability in the event of litigation. Absolutely nothing can ever shield you from some litigious person suing you because they get some sort of perverse pleasure from doing so. Professional litigants abound!

For an added layer of protection I publish under a Nevada- Registered Limited Liability Corporation (LLC). I also carry a substantial insurance "umbrella" policy, which is actually quite inexpensive. These are matters you should discuss with your attorney and Certified Public Accountant (CPA). (I create and manage all my LLCs at thecompanycorporation.com)

Of course if you are writing fiction such as romance novels as opposed to non-fiction "how to safely wire a house" your potential for legal exposure is greatly reduced!

CHAPTER 14

AMAZON PAPERBACK

PRINT-ON-DEMAND

For a self-publisher, Amazon's **CreateSpace** platform is by far the greatest invention since sliced bread and sex! When I first began to write books back in the early '70s, as a self-publisher I would have to print a few thousand book copies at enormous expense, and then literally go door to door to book stores to market it. This process was expensive, and frustrating.

It was always impossible to compete with the big publishing houses, or to interest thousands of libraries in shelving a single self-published book. Aside from the love of writing and the considerable ego trip of seeing one's name on a book cover, it was a good thing my wife had a real job!

This was true for decades. Things today are **TOTALLY** different. (And today my wife doesn't even **need** a real job!) This is the

Golden Age for the self-publisher! Through Amazon's print-on-demand platform it is possible for an independent ("Indie") publisher to reach an audience of hundreds of millions worldwide at ZERO cost, and virtually overnight! How traditional print-book publishers stay in business today I have not got a clue.

Let's start from scratch and publish a print-on-demand paperback book through CreateSpace, to be sold through Amazon.

For whatever reason, it is recommended that you use the Firefox web browser. Other browsers, particularly Google Chrome, are not as compatible with the CreateSpace platform uploads. If you do not have Firefox, just Google "Firefox download" and get a free copy. Then use it to access createspace.com, and open up a free account there. Then just follow the account-creation prompts, which are intuitive.

Once you have set up your account, log in. You will see "Start your New Project". Enter you book title, check "Paperback", and choose "Guided" for the uploads. Once the entire process becomes "second nature" the pro-quickie upload option might save you a minute or two. Hit "Get Started". You will then see a very intuitive four-part "dashboard":

"Set Up" includes your Title Information, ISBN, Interior, Cover and Complete Setup steps.

"Review" includes File Preview and Proof Your Book.

"Distribute" offers you six channels (you want them all), Pricing, Description, and Publish On Kindle.

"Sales & Marketing" allows you to Track Sales, use Marketing Services, and Get Ideas In "Resources".

Beginning with "Set Up", enter your title, author, and download your book description, which is the same you will use for your back-cover text. They allow you 4,000 characters for this description, so if you want to lengthen it beyond the back cover text (assuming you did the cover text first) do so. I never bother.

The text from my back cover is about one-quarter the allowable 4,000 character amount. Perhaps I am missing out on an opportunity to hype the book, but I believe if I did a good power-word-rich description on the back cover I really cannot add a lot more to it. If you choose to do this long description first you will need to write the shorter version for the cover, which to me is twice the work.

Next add your sub-title, then hit save and continue. Here is where you either enter an ISBN you bought from Bowker, or use/buy one of Amazon's numbers. Hit continue.

Next you choose your interior. The easiest, and least expensive to produce (most net profit for you) is "Black & White" as opposed to "Color", and "White" paper as opposed to "Cream" paper. (Your cover will always automatically be printed in full color.) If you start messing with color pictures within the book you make your book far more expensive to produce. It forces you to ask for a higher price, and lowers the number of copies you will sell. If you want pictures imbedded in your text and do not care that they print in black and white it is a non-issue.

For "Trim Size" I have found through experimentation (as well as the experience of other authors) that 6" X 9" is a perfect size for **all** of your books. (Though you will not be asked for this information, I use 16 point type for shorter books, and 14 point for longer ones. Using 16 point makes any book a bit thicker and thus more pages. Bigger is better in the mind of the buyer, but it is also a bit more expensive to produce yielding a few cents less profit.)

The next step is the most critical. If you do everything correctly to this point it will go very smoothly. You have various options for the upload file format. After much trial and error and agonizing over repeated rejections I have found the following process to work 100% of the time: Write your book in Microsoft Word. Then in Word go to "Page

Layout" > "Size"> adjust to 6" X 9", with 3/4 inch margins all around.   After you do this, proofread the resulting text to be certain all of the Chapters begin at the top of a page. This is the file you upload to CreateSpace by clicking "Browse", locating and opening the appropriate file, uploading the file, and waiting a few minutes while CreateSpace converts your 6"x9" .docx file into a their preferred .pdf. If I try to do the conversion to .pdf myself **before** I upload, for some reason it complicates the process. Do so at your own risk.

Here is where crossing one's fingers seems to help! They do give you the option of proceeding to the next step (your cover) while they are playing with your text. What you are hoping to see is a message that says: "Our Automated Print Check Didn't Find Any Issues". There is a God! (If there **are** issues they will explain them to you for correction. You don't want issues.)

You are now ready to "Launch Interior Review". The first time I did this I was blown away! There, on the screen, is your finished book, open facing pages, with the ability for you to flip through the entire volume one page at a time! Do so in order to be certain that none of your text is cut off at the edges in the final version.

If you see a message on the right side that refers to a possible problem with fonts just ignore it. As long as you wrote your book in a sans-serif font such as Ariel this message is irrelevant. I have never explored exactly what they are trying to say here, and ignoring it has never caused me any issue.

Now you go back and on the left side choose "Cover". You want to choose "Upload A Print-Ready .pdf Cover", the one you had Fiverr construct as a single rear/spine/front combination. You do not want "Professional Cover Design" unless you want to pay an arm and a leg for something over which you have no direct control. You also do not want "Build Your Cover Online". They do have a very fine free cover-design function, but you are VERY limited by the available templates and I found it not to be worth the bother. Use

Fotolia/Paint per Chapter 12. Upload your cover. Remember, they will provide you with a free bar code for the back cover, but you must have left them a space in which to print it.

Now click on "Submit Your Files For Review". You will then be taken to the "Distribution" page. You are automatically and at no cost enrolled in three distribution channels: Amazon.com, Amazon Europe, and Create Space Store. You are then presented with a $25.00 add-on if you want to include "Bookstores & Online Retailers" plus "Create Space Direct" and "Libraries & Academic Institutions". I am quite certain that over time the twenty-five bucks is a bargain, so I always go for it.

Go through the intuitive secure payment process using your credit or debit card for the $25.00, and if you have used an Amazon-assigned ISBN you are now in **all** six distribution channels. If, however, you have used your **own** ISBN you **cannot** be included in the Library+ channels. For that one distribution channel you **must** use an

Amazon-assigned ISBN. Because I use my own ISBNs, I open up a parallel CreateSpace account using a different email address exclusively for this special distribution channel. I must be very careful when I upload the text in that channel that I have **their** ISBN on the title page (they assign it before you upload your text and you must go back to your 6"x9" Word document, erase your own ISBN, and add theirs.) Now hit "Save and Continue".

You will be taken to the pricing page, where you must decide what you are going to charge for your print-on-demand paperback. I generally charge $10.00 more than for my ebook versions. You can have fun playing with the calculator they provide, which automatically populates your net royalty for various ways a customer might make a purchase. It also populates the same information in both British and Euro currencies. Incidentally, you can change your pricing at any time in the future.

IMPORTANT NOTE: Once your book is available, and you are advertising it, be

certain you promote only the link that gives you the greatest commission! This will be obvious from the populated calculator. You can find that exact link once the book is available for public purchase.

Next you will have the option of uploading the "Author's Bio" information. Here I use the long text from inside my book. They allow about five times as much text space as needed for your rear cover if you choose to use that text.

After this you will add "English" for the book language (or whatever language in which you are publishing) and your "Country of Publication", which for me is United States. You will next enter a publication date. I always use the date I am in the site, but if permitted you can leave this blank. Many feel that not stating a publication date makes your book "ageless".

Finally, you will be asked for keywords. Unfortunately you are only allowed a scant **five** keywords and keyword phrases. I use the top five most-searched relevant phrases according to Google. Because Amazon makes money when you make money it seems to me to be self-defeating for them to not allow you to enter far more keywords. I'm sure they have their reasons.

After completing this section you will be presented with a tempting: "Publish On Kindle" option. I never use it, preferring to do all of my Kindle publishing on separate kdp.amazon.com accounts. I tried doing Kindle once through CreateSpace and it just made it more complicated as far as I was concerned, and much harder to keep things separated for my accounting purposes. Feel free to try it both ways. I just ignore it.

Now click on "My Account", choose "Member Dashboard" and you will see Status: "In Progress". In about two days this will switch to "Available". Rejoice! This is your signal to buy some copies for friends and relatives, and to begin your serious marketing efforts.

What I especially like about CreateSSpace is the availability of a toll-free number and very courteous 24/7 service. (866-356-2154). You are connected very quickly to literate English-speaking consultants who are very knowledgeable and helpful.

Once you have all of your ducks lined up in a row the actual submittal process should take well under a half-hour. And when you order a book on Monday, do not be surprised if by Wednesday shiny new very professional-looking paperbacks appear in your mailbox. How they manage to print these books on-demand and ship them out seemingly the same day is yet another Amazon miracle! The books are printed at a facility in South Carolina.

Times have definitely changed. It is said that today at least as many ebooks are being sold as print books. The proliferation of ebook readers, Kindle, Nook, iPads and the like, has been a modern-day revolution! I find I sell more ebooks than print-on-demand books, but the higher net royalty on the paperbacks makes up for it.

It is important when publishing anything at CreateSpace to choose "Amazon Retail" as a sales channel. If you fail to do so your content will only be available through CreateSpace directly, which most shoppers do not recognize as an arm of the highly-trusted Amazon brand. You can also create your own eStore at CreateSpace, but you have to drive traffic to it as you would to any website. I never bother with that, but it may be worthwhile to try it.

Selling ebooks is overall more profitable, but there is something extremely ego-satisfying in seeing and feeling your masterpiece in the palm of your hand! A physical book with a great cover is certain to impress friends and family alike. **YOU ARE NOW A _PUBLISHED AUTHOR_**! **CONGRATULATIONS!!!** This sets you apart from most of the rest of the world's population.

And because your books stay "in print" forever, it gives you the potential for residual income for the rest of your life!

CHAPTER 15

PUBLISHING AMAZON KINDLE EBOOKS

The Amazon Kindle electronic ebook reader was a great success from the moment Oprah Winfrey glowed over it on her TV show. It has become the most popular such device, having sold tens of millions of units. Recently Amazon upgraded it with the Flame, which is able to display color images among other enhancements.

If you hope to be a successful self-publisher you simply must publish on Kindle Direct Publishing (KDP). They pay an incredibly high royalty, payout often, and provide you with the opportunity to market along with the number one bookseller on earth!

There is very little not to like about the Kindle website. The only item that is "tricky" is formatting your book in such a way that when a Kindle device owner downloads it they can click on a Chapter heading in your Table Of Contents (TOC) and be immediately taken to the start of that chapter!

As with the Smashwords conversion, I find it infinitely easier to spend five bucks at Fiverr.com and have someone, within a day, send me a file that I just upload to KDP and the clickable TOC works perfectly. Can you do it yourself and save five bucks? Absolutely. You can buy "clickable TOC" conversion software (also from people at Fiverr.com) that works quite well, and can find similar software with a Google search. I just find outsourcing it to Fiverr to be super-easy.

Amazon also has a conversion program on the Kindle website that you can download, but for the life of me I cannot get it to work on my computer.

Your first step is to set up your free account at kdp.amazon.com. Just follow the intuitive steps. Once you have an account set up you will be first shown an innocuous choice to join "KDP SELECT". **DO NOT JOIN IT!** It is an innovative program wherein authors can earn money for books that are "lent" rather than bought. I'm certain there are people who make some money with it. However, at this writing if you choose to participate in "KDP Select" Amazon insists on **EXCLUSIVITY** for everything Kindle! This means no Smashwords or any other off-Amazon marketing.

I read of many people who join KDP Select, innocently and unknowingly join Smashwords, and get a termination letter from Amazon! Just pass this choice by, unless in the future they lift this exclusivity restriction.

For all else on KDP exclusivity is not an issue. Were they to insist on exclusivity across the board I am certain (as I'm sure Amazon knows) that many authors might choose not to publish there. I have read in blogs that some authors feel they earn more money at Smashwords than at Kindle.

With your KDP account set-up out of the way, your will have a very direct and easy to use nine-step process to publish your book.

It can be accomplished easily within ten minutes once you have all of the require material ready to upload and have made some basic decisions. You will need:

A book description. If I'm happy with my book rear cover description I use it as is. If you want to greatly expand upon that length you can.

A list of only seven key words or phrases. Why they limit this list is beyond me, because the more ways a buyer can find your book the more books you will sell and the more money Amazon will make. They even limit the number of characters in the phrases!

The sample % you want to offer your potential buyer. This will vary from book to book. You need to allow the potential buyer to get far enough into the book to want to buy it, but not so far that they don't **need** to buy it!

The book price you want to charge.

The text of your book as a .doc file specially prepared at Fiverr to have a clickable Table Of Contents.

Your front cover .jpg file, adjusted to 1,000 pixels on the longside (easily done in Microsoft Paint).

Once you have all of this ready, Step 1 covers your book title, the description of the book, the author and any other contributors, the language in which your book is written, your publication date, the identity of the publisher, and an **optional** ISBN. You do not actually **need** an ISBN for an ebook, because its primary function is intended for cataloging printed books. (Smashwords, discussed in the following chapter, does require an ISBN because certain of their ebook distribution platforms use it for purposes of their own.)

Step 2 simply verifies that you have the publishing rights to your book. Step 3 lets you choose the search category and a secondary category, both from very complete drop-down menus. It is here where you enter your seven keywords or keyword phrases.

In Step 4 you upload the .jpg image of your front cover. Step 5 is where you upload the specially-prepared book contents including the clickable Table of Contents. Step 6 allows you to preview the book. This step is not automatically totally-functional in that it does not accurately simulate the Kindle Reader experience. You do, however, have the option of downloading a Kindle Reader Program to view your book as a buyer would see it and assure yourself that the TOC is indeed functionally clickable. I never bother.

In step 7 you list your distribution territory. Why anyone would click anything other than "Worldwide" I haven't got a clue.

In step 8 you indicate your royalty percentage. Because this is automatically set by your retail price I'm not sure why they offer this choice. Then you add your US$ price, and click a few boxes to see the price in other key currencies.

In Step 9 you indicate your "lend my book" preference, which I never check. I see no purpose to lending something I am trying to sell! Then you agree to the Amazon Terms & Conditions, click Save and Publish, and you are done! It is very intuitive, very clean and very fast. Your book then goes into a review category, which will switch to "LIVE" in a few days if everything you uploaded is AOK.

There is an interesting step you can take to set your title apart from others in Kindle. This step is adding "Book Extras" from Shelfari. "Shelfari" is an Amazon subsidiary. Adding "Shelfari Book Extras" to your book could increase its sales. What exactly is a Book Extra? It is a curated factoid that offers readers useful information while they're reading your book or deciding if they should buy your book!

This can help your book to stand from the crowd by providing character descriptions, important places, awards and a lot else to your book's metadata. In addition to appearing for free on Kindle's detail pages,

Kindle customers can access Book Extras directly.

To add "Book Extras" to your title, do the following:

Go to **shelfari.com**;

Log in using your Amazon.com username and password;

In the search bar, enter your title or author name;

Find your title in the search results;

Add, update or correct the community-contributed set of Book Extras designated for your title.

There is a lot of very useful information within the KDP website itself, and you should surely read all of it. To get your book up and published, however, simply following the above steps will get the job done.

Take as long as necessary to thoroughly study every aspect of the KDP site. If this takes you less than five hours you are not putting enough effort into the process!

Browse around. Drill deep. Observe and learn. Many Kindle books allow you to read part of the content. Do so. It can be a good learning experience.

Study the "Best Sellers" section. Look at both the "Top 100 Paid" and "Top 100 Free" titles. Study the Titles, the book covers, and the authors' descriptions. When you click on a book be certain to read the feedback section. Try to get a feel for what people think about different books, and why they rate them as they do in the one (worst) to five (best) "stars rating" system.

Check out the various categories on the side, especially focusing on those in which you may have some interest or special knowledge. All you are doing at this point is looking for IDEAS, and (hopefully) getting excited! Be sure to visit the Forums.

Write down at least five ideas for your own future books. The more ideas the better. Now you are ready to convert those ideas into cash.

The key is to get started! What might seem to you to be an impossible task at this point will become easier and easier as you actually get busy and start publishing!

It's Easy, It's fun, and it's profitable. What more could you ask for in a home based business?

CHAPTER 16
YOUR SMASHWORDS
EBOOK PLATFORMS

What is amazing about SMASHWORDS is the immense diversity and scope of their distribution. Most self-publishers such as myself find that a fairly decent portion of their ebook sales are derived here, even though Amazon's Kindle is by far the single most popular ebook reader. In fact, Kindle has become almost a generic term for an electronic book reader. Barnes & Noble, which is one of Smashword's many distribution platforms at this writing has made the news lately as discussing whether to drop their Nook reader entirely.

Smashwords also sells your ebooks directly from their own site. But once you have properly formatted your manuscript for inclusion in their "Premium Catalog" (not exactly an easy task!)your ebook will be available for purchase in places worldwide you've probably never even heard of!

Owners of the popular Apple iPhones and iPods will be able to buy your books through Stanza. Android devices can be used to purchase through Aldiko and Word-Player. The Barnes& Noble Nook Reader is covered, as well as Sony and the Diesel ebook store. International coverage is through Kobo. And the important library distribution is covered through Baker and Taylor's Axis 360 service and the blio.com store. That represents a lot of potential sales! So do not overlook publishing at Smashwords.

Go to smashwords.com and follow the intuitive instructions to open a free account. That's the easy part.

Before I proceed, let me tell you about a few things I dislike about Smashwords as compared with Kindle and CreateSpace.

First, there is no way you can contact them by phone if you have a question. You can send an email, but I challenge you to find the email address anywhere on the site in under a half-hour! (It is: mc@smashwords.com, deeply buried in obscure fine print). They respond fairly quickly, but their responses often do not answer my question on the first try. Very frustrating to say the least.

Second, the required book upload format is, at least for me, virtually impossible to create by myself. They have a "Style Guide" which is literally almost an **inch thick** when printed out! I have spent dozens of hours on three occasions trying to follow it to no avail. Were it not for people at Fiverr.com who have some magic way they do this quickly I would never attempt to publish at Smashwords.

Third, and perhaps the most annoying thing about the site, is the fact that it does not **retain** anything you input if you need to go back to fix something, or leave the site entirely to come back at a later time. If everything does not go through first shot, and it frequently does not for me, you have to start from scratch and input everything all over again. Seriously annoying.

Next, though this may not seem important, I find it irritating that when I add a new title I need to create a "ghost author" on a separate part of the website every time I use a pen name or a nickname, which is often. Then later on in the submittal process I need to remember to match it to the book title from a drop down list at the appropriate time. If I forget to do so, it defaults to the name used for the first book I published there. In the Amazon sites you just add the author of the book you are publishing right under the book title immediately after you enter it.

Fifth, but not least in the gripe category, often the site rejects my book manuscript upload and my cover upload as being "in an unacceptable format" when they are **positively 100% in conformity.** If you make enough attempts you can get it to work, but you can get an ulcer doing it. Sometimes just changing the **name** of the file you are uploading makes a difference. I have been unable to identify the problem.

I use three browsers: Microsoft Internet Explorer, Google Chrome, and Firefox. Each one shows a slightly different Smashwords website, and interacts differently with it. But there are times when I cannot get an upload "lock" with any of the three. They claim Chrome works best. I see no difference between the three....none work as well as I would like!

Lastly, they pay you your royalties quarterly and if the timing of your orders hits the calendar off-cycle, you might not see your royalties for a lot longer than that.

With all that said, I still think **it is important to publish at Smashwords** if you can endure the frustrations. For starters, get all of the following together before you start:

A 400 character short book description, which has to be created from the description on your back cover, which probably exceeds that size.

A 4000 character book description. If I'm happy with my book rear cover description I use it as is. If you want to greatly expand upon that length you can.

As large a list of key words as you want to find. You cannot cut and paste these. They must be entered one at a time, so I usually stop at the twenty with the highest Google traffic volume. There appears to be no limit. **This to me is a very significant plus over the Amazon sites which accept only a few keywords.**

The sample % you want to offer your potential buyer. You need to allow the potential buyer to get far enough into the book to want to buy it, but not so far that they don't **need** to buy it!

The book price you want to charge.

The text of your book as a .doc file specially prepared at Fiverr.

Your front cover .jpg file, adjusted to 1,400 pixels on the short side (easily done in Microsoft Paint).

Now once you have all of this together it **SHOULD** take you about ten minutes maximum to complete the upload. There are five steps, listed as Step 1 to Step 5.

Step 1 is your title, your short and long description, the language your text is in, and certification that your text has no sexual content.

Step 2 is your pricing and sampling. When you enter a price three pretty colorful pie charts appear showing how the retail prices is split up between you and Smashwords on different platforms. If the pie charts do not appear **instantly** STOP and re-login using a different browser. It is a certain sign that your later uploads will not work.

Step 3 consists of two drop-down category menus, which are quite complete. When you choose "non-fiction" or "fiction" a second drop-down menu should instantly appear. If it says "searching" don't bother to wait. You'll die of old age! It will never allow you to upload your text. This is the same situation as with the pie charts mentioned above. Re-login with another browser and start the whole darn process over from scratch.

Step 4 is your search tags. You must input these one at a time. It is tedious and the most time-consuming part of the whole process, because you can have so many of them. There's never a free lunch!

Step 5 is a list of formats into which Smashwords converts your book upload. Delete "Kindle". It is advantageous to do Kindle directly at Amazon KDP….if nothing else Kindle pays you more frequently.

Step 6 is the upload of your cover image. You must adjust the cover size to be 1,400 pixels on the short side and the keep the 6:9 ratio on the long side. This is very easily done in Microsoft Paint or any other image manipulation program.

Step 7 is the upload of your book text, in specially prepared format and as a .doc file.

Step 8 is your agreement with their Terms & Conditions.

Step 9 is where you connect a "ghost author", previously added elsewhere on the site, with the book title.

Now click **PUBLISH**. This is where I find it close to a miracle if everything is accepted. If the only problem is one of omission of some item, you can go back and add it without losing data. But if the problem is an "unacceptable format", you are screwed. You need to try again, uploading a differently-labeled but identical file. If this still does not produce an acceptance, you need to start from scratch in a different browser.

I have managed to publish many titles at Smashwords, but every one took far more time and aggravation than it should have. Compared to Amazon's platforms, it's a pain in the poop to use.

ALL I CAN SAY AT THIS POINT IS STAY PATIENT, BE PERSISTANT, AND **GOOD LUCK!!!! Your bank account will thank you.**

CHAPTER 17

<u>SOCIAL MEDIA MARKETING</u>

The number of individuals using social media platforms such as Facebook, MySpace, Twitter, YouTube and Pinterest is mind- boggling. It is well into the hundreds of millions! Internet self-publishers have found that properly used these platforms can drive serious traffic to a website or point-of-purchase for selling your books.

If you happen to be a social media whizz, and many of you today are, you have a great opportunity to promote your book to your followers. Facebook, MySpace, Twitter, YouTube and Pinterest, to name a few, are all great promotional tools **IF** you are accustomed to using them and are fortunate enough to have a large and loyal following. If you are more like me, and wouldn't know a tweet from a twit, a YouTube from a boob-tube or a Pinterest from Mount Everest, Fiverr is your salvation!

There are individuals on Fiverr who have countless followers at the various social sites and will blast out your book ad for five bucks. Some profess to reach millions! My experience here is excellent.

So if you are already a user of social media, and have thousands of followers, you have a real marketing advantage leg up over the social media wallflowers (such as I). It will be very easy for you to broadcast information about your book and interest people who know you on some level to actually **buy** your book. Perhaps even better, you could, if you wrote under a pen name, simply tell all of your friends and followers about this great new book you just bought and read and suggest they do likewise!

Should you not want to promote your book to your own network of followers, or even if you have no such network, this is **not a problem**. There is a wonderful alternative, and it costs very little. In fact, if you consider the cost/value of your time spent contacting all of your "friends" this alternative may look like the greatest bargain ever.

As I have suggested in this book for other purposes (and no, I am not in any way connected with them except as a buyer of their services) look to fiverr.com for your social site marketing help. Log in to fiverr.com, enter "advertise on Facebook" (or whichever media) in their search-function box, click "go", and you will find individuals with thousands, even millions, of friends and followers to whom they will broadcast your message **for five bucks!**

Your job is to craft a compelling short ad, the same as you would do for an online classified or an eBay listing. Then just upload it to your chosen fiverr-person and watch those sales figures grow!

Of course it is difficult to accurately track the results from any one social media ad broadcast. If you pay for one ad broadcast and suspend other marketing, and in the next few days your sales spike up dramatically, it is a pretty good bet that it was five dollars very well spent! I suggest you do this with **every** fiverr-person advertising this service in order to get maximum social-media coverage. This is sort of a no-brainer. It's easy, fast, inexpensive, and can make you a lot of money.

Remember, if each five-dollar broadcast sells just **one** of your books you'll be ahead of the game at the $9.97 price!

That's a pretty darn low break-even point.

CHAPTER 18

MARKETING

FIVERR BEYOND SOCIAL

In the last Chapter we looked at Social Media using fiverr.com as one way to promote your books. The Chapters that follow this one go into some detail about the various other kinds of marketing you can employ to enhance your sales. These include: press releases; article directories; on-line classified ads; eBay; Craigslist; blogs; forums; mini-websites; Google AdWords; and conventional classified advertising. The hard fact is that writing your book, and getting it published at the three major platforms, is only **one part** of the process of making a living as a writer.

Publishing is the ego satisfying part. Marketing is the wallet satisfying part.

There is bad news and good news. The bad news is you can do all of the above marketing 100% yourself. It's FREE, but time is money, so "free" is a relative term. The good news is that you can hire others to do the bulk of your marketing for very little money.

Fiverr.com is God's gift to the self-publisher. Aside from saving you endless hours formatting text and creating covers, you can find a "fiverr-person" to do just about anything in marketing you might need done, for just five bucks! I discussed Fiverr in some detail in Chapters 3 and 17. But marketing is so very important that there is much more to say about what you can have done there for a pittance.

You can find individuals to write press releases and articles about your book, and then place them appropriately. There are professional book reviewers. There are mini-website creators galore. There are Fiverrs who will run radio ads on local stations that they control. There are others who will write your ads and professionally create the spoken words for you. In fact, I doubt whether you can think of any promotional vehicle that some person on Fiverr cannot perform in your behalf.

Of course there is always elance.com and rentacoder.com for you to send out any task imaginable for bids if you do not find Fiverr to be adequate for your needs..

When you read the Chapters that follow you will get a feel for what is involved in doing all manner of marketing yourself. You may choose to do it all yourself, and save money. But as I said before, the old bromide "Time Is Money" is absolutely true. While someone else is doing your marketing you could be creating your next money-making book! Only you can decide the best marketing path for you to take, and the optimum use of your valuable time.

For internet entrepreneurs, I can tell you with 100% certainty that there is a direct relationship between how much one uses outsourcing for a wide variety of self-publishing-related tasks and how much money one nets. The judicious use of others' sweat can make your life easier and your wallet fatter. If you try to do everything yourself you can easily become discouraged.

Writing and self-publishing for profit can be fun. I cannot think of anything I would rather do for a living (except perhaps being a golf pro, but that's another story). If I had to format my books myself, create my own full covers, and tweet my way to success, I truly would hate my work and find something else less frustrating to occupy my time!

To summarize, outsourcing the following tasks can put more money in your pocket:

Writing and distributing Press Releases;

Writing and posting articles in directories;

Following and writing blogs;

Participating in forums;

Advertising on eBay and Craigslist;

Creating mini-websites;

Creating and placing conventional ads.

The following Chapters will explain these tasks in some detail.

CHAPTER 19

MARKETING

YOUR PRESS RELEASES

So now you've written your book, and finally see that it is available to the public in print-on-demand and every imaginable ebook format. Now at long last you can sit back and collect your royalties and live happily ever after, tight? **NOT** right! The fact is, now that your ego is all tingly, your real work to make some money has just begun.

Sit back and do nothing and you will probably sell a few books. Very few. The sad fact is that many very excellent books never sell a single copy without a real marketing effort on the part of the author.

If the book you have written is newsworthy (fingers crossed) then the most important element of your "let's make some money" marketing is the **press release**.

Though you may be a writing genius, press releases are not the place to re-invent the wheel or display your intuitive literary prowess. There is a very specific format that **MUST** be followed if you hope to have your press release end up anywhere other than the trash bin. There are guidelines to follow. Follow them exactly! Keep in mind that editors are deluged with press releases. Why in the world should they accept, or even read, yours? You can greatly increase your odds of press release success by following a number of hard and fast rules.

One cardinal rule is to make your press release technically perfect. No misspelled words. No lousy English. No "all capital" words. No slang. No technical terms. Write only as a "third party": no "we", "us", "ours; only "they", "them", "theirs". And remember this is NOT an advertisement as such, it is **information.**

Not interested in crafting your own press releases? Then pay for someone else to do it. Just make certain they follow the guidelines presented below. You can try fiverr.com and probably find someone who will do a decent job for five bucks. Or you can use elance.com or rentacoder.com and put the job out for bids. Some of the press release companies will write one for you for a rather steep price.

Now that we have the above basics out of the way, let's look at the "carved in stone" formats, irrespective of whether you write the press releases yourself or pay someone else to do it.

By far the **best**, and **by far** the most time consuming, is direct-addressed snail-mail press releases sent to Editors of various newspapers. There is a set of rules here that is a bit different from using on-line press release companies for your distribution. The key rules to follow are:

Address standard business envelopes by hand to the news organization's mailing address directly to the Editor by name. (I always mark the envelope "Personal and Confidential").You get this personal address information from: "usnpl.com/addr/". You can use standard first-class postage, Priority Mail, or even Express Mail, though the latter two choices get rather expensive if you are sending out press releases to a lot of editors.

Enclose a **single** 8½ x 11 sheet of paper, typed in your word processor in Arial font (or any "sans-serif" font), **double spaced** (so the Editor can write in notes between the lines). <u>That is your entire press release.</u> This forces brevity, and is much more difficult to craft than the longer-text press releases permitted on line. One sheet, easily read, short and sweet. For the press release text itself, follow closely everything shown below. You just have to shorten it all down to the "meat".

There is one possible exception to snail-mail, but it is ONLY for press releases to radio stations. Here, send your one-page press release by FAX instead of mailing it. **<u>NEVER</u>** <u>email a press release to anyone in any media.</u> That is a 100% guarantee it will not be seen. (Even if your headline is: "An Alien Just Landed In My Yard and I Have Him Captive In My Basement" or "Jesus

Returned And HE Is Sitting In My Living Room!" it won't escape the SPAM filter!)

There is a slight physical variant for the snail-mail-direct or FAXed press release. In the upper left corner write "For Immediate Release". In the upper right corner put your name, email address and phone number.

In all of your press releases use natural left-justified line wraps as you see in this book.

There are **SEVEN** separate and distinct parts to any press release. Follow them all in order. These are: **Headline; Summary; Dateline; Starting Paragraph; Details; Boilerplate, and Media Contact Information.** All are important, but the Headline is most important, followed in importance by the Summary, and the Starting Paragraph.

First, **THE HEADLINE:**

Absolutely **nothing** is more important to your press release success than your headline. This is one single line of text that tells what your press release is all about. It

MUST catch your reader's attention. It must be interesting, or exciting, or controversial, or all three. <u>You sell the benefits of your book in the headline.</u> If possible it can be written in the form of a question. If it can be about something that is currently newsworthy all the better. If possible it should contain a keyword or two. Capitalize ONLY the first letter of each word (except "to", "of", "the" and similar short words.)

But here's the rub: your headline needs to be **SHORT**! Google only allows 60 characters in a headline. Yahoo allows 120. Certain press release companies allow as many as 170 characters. The recommended optimum is **80 characters**. This can be a challenge to create. Spend as much time on your headline as on all other parts of the press release combined.

Second, **THE SUMMARY**

This is where you "sell" your press release to the journalist. This must be a single paragraph and can be one to four sentences. The idea is to capture attention in 250 characters or less! Don't give too much information....you want them to read on!

Third, **THE DATELINE** (use one unless you are instructed not to by one of the press release companies who add their own.)This is the city in which you or your company is located, followed by the release date. Example: "New York, N. Y. August 15, 2012"

Fourth, **THE OPENING PARAGRAPH**

This is a critical item, second only to your headline. This paragraph is the key. It's where you keep 'em or lose 'em. It should be 175 to 300 words long, though fewer words is best. It's the "who", "what", "when", "where" and "why" of your book. If possible tie it in with current events or trends or social issues. Create urgency and importance. Use powerful verbs, key words, and power words. Provide the reader with **useful information**. It's a good idea to work your company name in here.

Fifth, **THE DETAILS**

This is the body of your story. It should be two paragraphs of five to eight lines each. A total of 500 words or 3,000 characters is considered optimal. Some press release companies allow up to 8,000 characters, so it is a good idea to prepare different versions of your press release to satisfy the requirements of different companies. Here is the opportunity to restate and summarize the key points of your overall release.

Timeliness of your information is very important. Somehow work in why you are announcing this press release at this particular time, for example, "We just published…….".

Avoid exclamation points, and hyperbole such as "amazing".

<u>Sixth,</u> **THE "ABOUT"**

This is "boilerplate" that you should have created for other purposes. This is background information on the company or individual issuing the press release. Be brief and specific, one or two lines.

Seventh and last, **MEDIA CONTACT INFORMATION**

Name, organization, phone and FAX numbers, email address, website address, and mailing address

OVERALL, your press release should be within 300 and 800 total words. Do not forget to refer to the **keywords** lists you created earlier, and to the lists of **power words** in Chapter 8. The more of both that you can work into your copy without affecting its natural flow the better.

At the bottom center of your press release put ### (three pound signs) which signifies "The End" and lends a professional touch!

Creating a dynamite press release is an art and requires a lot of practice. The length restraints are the most difficult around which a writer must work. You will find that it takes a **lot** of practice. Over time though the process becomes second nature.

The following is a list of press release companies you should explore in detail. Go to each website. Sign up for a free account. Drill down into all of the information on the site. Many have excellent "How To Write A Press Release" dissertations. Then decide which "free" press release offers to use, and what level of paid-for releases fits your budget. These are listed in no particular order:

prlog.com

pr.com

prnewswire.com

prweb.com

i-newswire.com

eworldwire.com

24-7pressrelease.com

1888pressrelease.com

The above eight are the ones where I maintain accounts. If you do a Google search you will find many dozens of others you might want to join. Many have free press release programs with limited releases, but you can't beat the price!

Again, check out "Press Releases" at fiverr.com. You will find dozens of individuals who specialize in both writing and submitting press releases. It is difficult not to try a few of these at five bucks a pop!

CHAPTER 20
MARKETING
ARTICLE DIRECTORY MAGIC

Perhaps the single most powerful and FREE approach to making book sales is called "Article Marketing". Each week submit one short article (250 -350 words is a good range) on your niche topic. Do not write this as "sales copy". Make it informative in some valuable way.

Never try to pitch your company or product in the article itself. Article directories are looking for information, not promotion. You want interesting articles that people will read to the very bottom where they will find your profile and your link to someplace that makes you money.

Once written you must submit your articles to some "article directories". When website owners and ezine publishers want free useful information-rich material to reprint they turn to the article directories.

For getting this free content they agree not to alter your article in any way. Most important they must leave your resource box, which you placed at the end of your article (with the link to your website or your ebook or print-on-demand offer or download) exactly as you wrote it.

A Google search for "Article Directories That Allow Links" turns up 242 million results! You do not need quite that many. The following two are the "must list on these" list. Google seems to favor them.

ezinearticles.com (By far the biggest, but you must link to a squeeze page or pre-sell content website page. Many smaller directories will spider-search this site and place your article on their site as well.)

usfreeads.com (Not exactly an article site, but you can link directly to your website.)

The following are excellent additional directory choices:

affsphere.com
goarticles.com
articlecity.com
articlesbase.com
articledashboard.com
articlesfactory.com
newfreearticles.com
sitepronews.com

Keep in mind that some of these article directories get tens of thousands of visitors every day. When someone uses your article, others to whom they send it might also use it. This is known as "viral marketing", because your article with its links spreads like a virus across the internet!

The word "viral" carries the negative "virus" connotation. No one wants to be sick. No one wants their computer to be sick. For these reasons I prefer to use the term: **"Auto-Effective Marketing"** whenever referring to "viral" marketing techniques.

Other useful article directory choices are:

articlecube.com

articlealley.com

articlesnatch.com

easyarticles.com

articlebiz.com

theleadingarticles.com

isnare.com

hubpages.com

technorati.com

buzzle.com

brighthub.com

thefreelibrary.com

suite101.com

ideamarketers.com

ezau.com

contentcrooner.com

distributeyourarticles.com

articleclone.com

articlegems.com

findarticles.com

Many article site owners do not want you posting duplicate content that you posted to other similar sites. Always read the "Terms and Conditions" and/or "Article Guidelines", and follow them.

In general, once you submit an article it usually takes about a week to appear on the first page of search results. It will remain there a month or two. **I suggest you submit at least four new articles every day if you hope to make this business model a primary source of internet income.**

There are also over **150** specialized article directories that focus on a **single** topic or niche. Have a product related to dogs? Post an article in: bestdogarticles.com. How about hair care? See: haircarearticles.com. Product related to college? Check out: youronlinecollegeguide.com. Do a search on Google for "Specialist Article Directories" and you will find one on just about any imaginable topic.

Your resource box, which is your earnings-key, placed at the end of your article, should look something like this:

"To learn more about (your niche product) check out my website at (your domain name). Here you will find many more tips on (your niche product). Feel free to distribute this article in any form you choose as long as you include this resource box. "

There is the MAJOR ancillary benefit to using the Article Directories. Many of those listed above have high Google Page Ranks. (You can find the Google Page Rank [PR] of any website by installing the Google Toolbar at toolbar.google.com). Back-links to your website from a PR 5 or higher website will increase your search engine ranking considerably, which can add to your traffic and ultimately to increased sales and revenue.

Instead of spending the time to post your articles to each directory yourself you can pay a nominal sum to have someone else do it for you. There are many directory submission vendors. One with which I am familiar is at: seoster.com. Check it out. They have many plans available. For example, for under $20 they will submit your article to 100+ high page rank directories.

If you do a Google search for "Directory Submission Tools" you will find that there are many software programs available for purchase that you can install yourself and do mass submissions of your articles to directories. You may find that some of these are cost effective.

IDEAS FOR ARTICLES

There are at least a dozen "article categories" you can exploit and relate to your books and reports. Within these categories you can create infinite variations:

1.Answer A Question. "What Does xxxxxxx Mean?". "xxxxxxx Answered at Last!". "What Does It Mean When Someone

Says xxxxxx". "Why would someone xxxxxxxx".

2.How To: "How To Prevent xxxxxxx". "How To Build A Better xxxxxxx". "How To Get Rid Of xxxxxx In A Week!".

3.Hot Trends: "Top Five Trends In xxxxxxx." "3 Super-Hot Trends In xxxxxxx." "Are You Missing These Three Trends In xxxxxxx."

4.Free: "5 Places To Get Free xxxxxxx." "Why Pay For xxxxxxx When You Can Get It For Free?" "3 Places To Get Free xxxxxx For Your xxxxxxx".

5.Cheap: "3 Ways To Get Cheap xxxxxx". "Five Of The Cheapest xxxxxxx". "Are You Missing The 7 Cheapest xxxxxx?".

6.Easy/Fast: "Seven Easy Ways To xxxxxx". "Don't Struggle. Use these three easy ways to xxxxxx". "Five Of The Fastest xxxxxx". "3 Ways To Get Faster xxxxxx".

7.Avoid Problems And Pain: "3 Ways To Avoid The xxxxxx Trap". "Never Do This If You Want xxxxxx". "7 Things Not To Do If You Want xxxxxx."

8.Reviews: Thinking Of Buying xxxxxx? Read This First". "xxxxxx And xxxxxx Compared Side By Side." "Should Beginners Buy xxxxxx". "Is xxxxxx Really User-Friendly?".

9. Rules, Laws, Principles: "The 7 Laws Of xxxxxx". "Three Success Rules Of xxxxxx". "Do You Know The 5 Basic Principles Of xxxxxx".

10. Top Tips: "7 Top Tips For Avoiding xxxxxx". "Five Top Tips For Better xxxxxx". "Do You Know The Top Three Tips For xxxxxx?".

11. Experts: "3 Ways The Experts xxxxxx". "What The Experts Recommend For xxxxxx". "5 Expert Tactics For xxxxx".

12. X vs Y: "Should You Buy xxxxxx or xxxxxx?". "xxxxxx vs xxxxxx, Which Is Best?". "Why Is xxxxxx Better Than xxxxxx?

Still need an idea for an ezine or article? Google search the keyword "TIP". This will give you a wealth of ideas. Add these three words: "learn", "training" and "buy" to open up a Pandors's box of book and report writing possibilities. Be sure to write books that are timeless. Avoid current events. You want your material to be bought and read for years to come.

The following is a list of ezines (electronic on-line magazines)that accept advertising. You can get many ideas for your own ezine ad solicitations from studying these:

Ezinehits.com/ad-rates.htm

Thegurumarketer.com/ad-rates.htm
Goldbar.net/advert.html
Gmhnewsletter.com
Workathomenews.com/advertising.html</a>
Bizweb2000.com/ads.htm</a>
Inetexchange.com/inet-mailer.html
Themoneymakingaffiliates.com/advertise
Netincomesite.com/ezineadrates/ezineadrat
es.htm
Superpromo.com/optadorder.html
Rimdigest.com/ads.html</a>
Topliving.com/marketing/fmailing.htm</a>

You can go to ezinesearch.com for a
comprehensive list of ezines that accept
advertising.

CONCLUSIONS

Of all of the possible FREE ways to promote
your books while obtaining quality website
backlinks, using popular Article Directories is
one of the easiest and most profitable. Be
certain to focus a significant amount of time
on this one of many possible ways to

promote your books. You won't be sorry that you did.

And remember, there is always a Fiverr-person waiting in the wings to do everything for you for five bucks! **JUST DO IT!**

CHAPTER 21
<u>MARKETING WITH</u>
<u>BLOGS AND PINGS</u>

Among the many ways you can promote your books and earn more royalties, blogging is high on the list in terms of effectiveness. If you are already a "blogger" this chapter may seem a bit too basic for you. But for those to whom blogging is a whole new world this chapter may seem a bit complicated. In fact, of all the suggested marketing methods, this is the one that will take you the most time to learn. I won't be insulted if you skip it!

In the overall marketing scheme of things, you surely must begin with press releases and article posting. Involvement with social media is also very important. A highly visible blog-oriented website on which you can sell your books directly or direct buyers to Amazon and Smashwords is, however, potentially a good source of customers.

To the uninitiated, "Blogging & Pinging" sounds like a law firm or a music group! It is in fact a great way to get search engine recognition and to attract those critical visitors to your website.

"Blog" is short for "We**bLog**". It is your personal and often-updated journal (log) intended for public consumption. "Pinging" is a method of informing others that your blog exists, and alerts them whenever you make a new blog posting.

When we talk about blogs here we have two separate topics to consider. One is creating websites directly with blogs using Google's "Blogger" program. The other is creating websites using a blog-based software program called "Word Press". There are other blog software choices, but these two have become industry standards.

GOOGLE'S BLOGGER PLATFORM

Let's first talk "Blogger". A blog is a combination of a database and a website. You focus on written content, while Blogger dates and archives your entries any way you wish (or not at all). The website it generates can contain not only your latest blog, but links to all previous blogs. It can contain photos as well as written copy. It can contain videos. It can contain, if you wish, a mechanism for visitors to leave comments.

In general, creating a book-marketing website in the conventional manner, at your website's host's servers, can be a challenge. This is especially true the first time you do it. In time you will find that is really not particularly difficult.

Although most web hosts have control panels (known as "cPanels") to facilitate website creation there is a rather steep learning curve. If you were to print out (as I have) all of the cPanel instructions you would end up with hundreds of pages of text almost an inch thick! A bit intimidating to say the least.

The key to creating book promotion websites quickly and easily is using Google's FREE blogging platform found at: blogger.com.   Starting your blog is amazingly simple. Create your account at blogger.com by filling in some forms with basic preferences. Then chose one of their many templates, and you are ready to boogie! Or bloggie. Or whatever.

Blogger even hosts your website for FREE on its BlogSpot servers, in exchange for tolerating a small amount of their advertising. But you <u>can</u> host your blog at your own web host of choice if you prefer. Personally I want total control of my business websites now and evermore so I choose never to have Google as my web host. But that does cost me hosting fees, and you can't beat Free.

Blogger and BlogSpot are two different and distinct Google services. If the only purpose for your blog is to keep friends and family informed about your publishing exploits then the free BlogSpot hosting is perfect for your needs.

Sign up at blogger.com. For starters you will want to strip the blog template totally bare, all white. Then you open the "html editor" and paste in your message. That is all there is to it!

You type your post in the main editing area. You can click "Preview" to see how it will look once published. It is automatically formatted with the template you chose. Their entire website is intuitive and easy to navigate. Once you have used it the first time, it becomes extremely easy in the future. Very flat learning curve compared to a cPanel.

Remember, by using Blogger you are using a Google product, and they really prefer it over other blogging software. Using Blogger greatly enhances your Google search engine ranking. Google likes it even better if you make a new blog post to your site at least once a week. All search engines reward unique, **changing** content.

The big advantage of blogging and pinging is that it gets your website indexed by the search engines almost immediately. And again, it's FREE.   The more people that can find your website the more books you will sell and the more money you will earn.

The above is an over-simplified look at Blogger. If you are creating a blog simply for personal use between family and friends that is about all you need to know. But blogging for business purposes, setting up an effective marketing blog, is very different from creating a social blog.

Social blogging is sort of an extended version of the character-limited Twitter mini-blog. You do not have to be concerned about using the optimal keywords, search engine optimization, or getting noticed and ranked by the search engines. It is extremely easy to create a social blog in Blogger.

Blogging for business purposes is NOT extremely easy to accomplish. But neither is it rocket science. It is almost impossible to get it right without some trial and error unless you have a good set of instructions. I hope to share with you here my experiences which hopefully will save you a great deal of time and angst.

BEFORE you ever consider creating your business blog website there are many preliminary things you need to do. Without these initial steps you will find yourself going back and making changes in your entries in Blogger time and time again. In fact you won't have a clue what information to fill into many of the boxes.

If you are already running a non-blog-based business and have books being marketed elsewhere you can skip to the highlighted paragraph below to where we first access the Blogger program.

First, create a list of the ten best keywords related to the content of your book, as discussed in Chapter 11.

Now you must register your keyword-rich domain name related to your book's topic. Next choose a web host to accept your Blogger program. This host should (and most do) have a program called "Technorati" installed.

Next you need to pretend you are writing a classified ad. Create headlines, sub-headlines, and short copy. We'll discuss setting up the necessary Yahooi! Account below.

NOW you have everything you need to begin to actually set up your Blogger website account.

Setting up this Google Blogger website correctly is a three-step process, Google is Step One, Yahoo! Step Two, and other blog search-engines step three.

Step one: Go to blogger.com. You can skip the "quick tour" until after you read this entire chapter, by which time you shouldn't need it! You will be asked for a "user name and password" and a "display name". This display name is shown at the end of each post you make.

For a social-only blog (family and friends) it is irrelevant what you fill in here. Not so for your book-selling business account. (Incidentally, you can change the "display name" for each and every blog you send in the future.)

Your "Title" should be short and sweet, three to four words maximum, and must contain your main keywords. (For a social blog it can simply be your name or nickname). Your URL will be: "(your keywords).blogspot.com".

Use a REAL email address where asked, and agree to the Terms of Service. It is not a bad idea to actually read these occasionally!

Time to name your blog, in the "Blog Title" box. Use two to four of your best keywords. In the next box choose your URL with the same keywords. If the URL you choose is already in use Google will tell you this. Try the hyphenated version, or no spaces between words, or rearrange the words, or try different words. You will eventually find an unused relevant URL.

If you choose to use Google's free BlogSpot hosting option (which I suggested above that you not do for a business website) your

BlogSpot address (URL) will be: (your keywords).blogspot.com. (At this point you can tell Blogger if you want to host outside of BlogSpot and they will explain how to accomplish this.)

Once you have your blog title and blog address, copy the verification letters (used by webmasters to weed out robot visitors) and click "continue".
You now choose one of a dozen or so ready-made templates for your blog. Always clear everything extraneous off the template and start on a clean white page. For all practical purposes it makes no difference which template you choose. Pick one you like.

Then click "continue" and you are ready to blog! Do a test blog, titling it "test". Leave the link field blank. Put "test" in the body of the post. Click "Publish Post".

If you click "View Blog", up it comes with your blog body text "test"! You will see four tabs across the top: "Posting", "Settings", Template" and "View Blog".

Click on "Settings". A number of sub-tabs drop down. You <u>must </u>make changes in some of these sub-tabs. <u>Leave everything else alone.</u>

Click on "Publishing". Where it says: "Notify Weblogs.com" you must make this choice: "Yes". Click on "Save Settings".

Click on "Formatting". At the bottom where it says "Show Link Field" you must make this choice: "Yes". Click on "Save Settings".

Click on "Comments". For "Who Can Comment" choose "Anyone". Under "Comment Notification Address" put any email address where you want notice that someone has posted a comment on your blog. (Incidentally, comments are great because they qualify as "new content" for the web-searching spiders.) Click on "Save Settings".

You want your blog to be archived daily. Make this change and click "Save Settings".

Under the "Site Feed Tab" make a note of your "Site Feed URL" which is your Blogger URL followed by "/atom.xml". Now click on the "Republish" button. Hopefully you will see: "Your blog published successfully." Everything is now set up properly for you to blog and ping!

Under the "Template" tab, your business blog template "Editor" entry each post should contain a keyword or phrase.

Under "Computer Security" you will see HTML code. Scroll down to: <p class="post-fiiter">. Below that, where you see: <aref="<**$BlogItemPermalinkURL$**>"title=" permanent link>< $BlogItemDateTime$></a></em>. Replace ONLY the highlighted words with your keywords. You need to do this for every blog you post.

You will often be using "BlogThis! in Blogger to cut and paste whole articles or parts of articles that relate to your book and website's content. You can add text and remove text by accessing the "HTML" (HyperTextMakeupLanguage) code (the body of the post) and making text changes within the code.

You do not need to actually know HTML code. Just look for the words you want to delete, or look for the position within the text where you want to insert additional words.

It is also important to have links on your blog, the more the better. Go to the "Templates" tab and scroll down to the HTML code for sidebar links. The yellow shaded code is the URL for the link. The green shaded code is what your visitor sees.

You want to have that green code be full of keywords. You replace ONLY the words

"EDITME" with your blog's URL (yellow area) and relevant keywords (green area).

You will see an "About Me" line in small type at the upper right. You will want to change the "Editor" in the sidebar to be the same as you are using when posting blogs. Replace: <$**BlogMemberProfile**$> with that name.

Last but not least go to the "Settings" tab and click on the "Basic" sub-tab. Put in a keyword rich description. Then click on "Save Settings" and "Republish".

All of this may seem like an awful lot of work, and at first it is. The more you blog the easier it all becomes, until it is second nature and takes relatively little time.

BLOGGING WITH YAHOO!

Now we come to the important **step two**, blogging and pinging Yahoo!. Setting this up properly is a bit tricky, and is where many Blogger sites go wrong. Yahoo! could well account for 30% of your website's income, so it is worthwhile to get this correct.

Go to yahoo.com and click on "My Yahoo" at the upper right. Click on "Sign Up" and follow the instructions to "Create Your Yahoo ID". This will be the address for your shiny new Yahoo email account (after checking the box "Create my free Yahoo! email account"). You will also create a case-sensitive password. (No need to mess with the "Customizing Yahoo!" option).

Copy the verification code. Agree to the Terms and Conditions (which I suggest you actually read). Once you click "I Agree" you are ready to link your blog website to your Yahoo account. The key is that Yahoo! allows you to subscribe to your OWN blog RSS feed.

FYI, "RSS", depending on who you ask, stands for "RDS Site Summary", "Rich Site Summary", or "Really Swift Syndication". Whatever.

Once you see your "Registration Completed" welcome page, print out a copy for your records. Click on "Continue To My Yahoo!". Up comes your own personal landing page. It is unimportant how you wish to personalize this page.

Now the key step, registering for your own blog. Click on the "Add Content" button at the very bottom of the landing page. Up comes a "Find Content" box. At the far right in almost zero point type (!) there is a link that says "Add RSS by URL". Click on it. Enter your Blogger **site feed** URL address, which is your Blogger URL followed by "/atom.xml". Click "Add".

The test post "text" you did earlier allows your blog to become "active" as Yahoo! does a quick search to validate your address. You will now see a screen with a button that reads: "Add To My Yahoo!". Click on it.

Once you see that your site feed URL has been accepted, click on the "My Yahoo! Home" button. You will see your blog listed at the bottom. Success is yours!!!

Yahoo! spiders have seen your site immediately upon receipt of your blog. They visited and indexed and you are on your way to search engine recognition with no delay at all.

Now let's ping Yahoo. Right-clicking on the blog you want to ping to Yahoo! you will see a box that reads: "Properties for (your blog name)". There will be a filled-in "Location" field containing your actual URL.

To ping Yahoo! you **must** add a string of text immediately before your URL in this box. Add the following code: "api.my.yahoo.com/rss/ping?u=", without the quotation marks. Ping Yahoo by clicking on the bookmarked link. Done.

You should see a message that says: Refresh requested: (your URL). To confirm that Yahoo! pinged the blog go back to your Yahoo! home page. At the bottom where you registered your blog earlier you should see the latest post. End of messing with Yahoo!.

In summary, every time you add content to Google's Blogger you will ping both Yahoo! and Ping-O-Matic. You may also wish to add your blog to other sites for submission. A Google search for "Blogging Submission Sites" will turn up many. You might want to start with: blogarama.com, blogsearchengine.com, and globeofblogs.com.

AND THE OTHERS...........

Last **step, three**. Let us now ping other search engines by using Technorati. This is a real-time every-minute-update that keeps track of the entire world of blogs, which is known affectionately as "The Blogosphere".

Go to technorati.com and click "Sign Up!".
Fill out the intuitive form. Scan down to the
"Your Blogs" section. Add your actual
Blogger (or non-Blogger) URL.

Next click on "Claim This Weblog". Copy the
code you see in "Profile Link" and include it
in a short blog post on your website. (The
text in this case need not be for visitor
consumption, but simply for pinging search-
purposes.) Then click on "Ping Technorati"
and wait for the "Ping Received" message,
and you are done.

There is a time-saver available.   Say you
have several new blogs, and might find
going through the above procedure for each
one to be a pain. Enter "Ping-O-Matic".
This service not only automatically pings
Technorati but a dozen or more other blog
search engines.   Go to pingomatic.com.

Enter your keyword-rich blog name created
earlier, and your Blogger or non-Blogger
URL. Check off every one of the "Services

To Ping" and click "Submit Pings". Done.
Bookmark this site and in the future return
here to re-ping quickly.

To be certain that your pinging is successful,
and your website is being spidered by the
web bots go to google.com and enter:
allinurl:(your URL). If you get "no results"
you are not yet being spidered. Check
every day for three days, and if you are still
not being spidered (unlikely) repeat the
entire pinging procedure.

Remember, without pinging every time you
blog it can be months before your website is
found by the search engine robot spiders.
Also, your website will only be re-spidered
and updated maybe every three months.
For optimum search engine placement
pinging after each blog post is critical.

In the future you will be using the "Blog This"
tab in Blogger. From the list of your
websites at the upper right side drop-down
menu you select one, and highlight some

text. Paste it into the body of your blog template. Note that your title has appeared in the Title Field, and your URL appears in the URL field. Also, the text you highlighted will be seen in the body of the blog. That's all there is to it!

From a marketing perspective one value of blogs is that you can easily place "contextual" (within your written copy) links in your blog. These can take your reader anywhere, including to a squeeze page on your website to collect email addresses, your website Buy It Now button to sell your .pdf book file, or directly to the purchase links at Amazon or Smashwords. You simply underline the text words that are the link, and tell Blogger what the URL is for that link.

You can get visitors to you blog website in all of the ways you get visitors to any other conventional website.

WORD PRESS YOUR WAY TO SUCCESS

Now let's turn our attention to the other popular blog software, creating your book marketing websites using a program called "WordPress". The advantage WordPress has over creating your websites within your web host's cPanel (or whatever site-creation program they may have) is a greatly flattened learning curve. And WordPress is FREE.

Just as with Blogger, you can have WordPress host your website, at wordpress.com. I do not recommend this. As with BlogPost, I greatly prefer to always be in full control of my website's future. I'm just more comfortable having my own host whose primary business is hosting.

The learning curve for a cPanel is rather steep. I downloaded and printed out the complete cPanel instructions once and ended up with a document having a few hundred pages almost an inch thick! That's all pretty intimidating, especially to someone new to the internet and website creation.

Once you have created a few websites within your host account using cPanel it becomes much easier, but that first website can be a real struggle.

WordPress on the other hand is relatively easy to work with. The power of the program lies in the large number of available "plug-ins" that enhance the functionality of this blog-based website-creation platform.

Have your domain name set up at some web host. Be certain your host is WordPress friendly by having "Fantastico" software; most are. You will go to wordpress.org (not .com) website and download the software to your host's server.

The WordPress folk pride themselves in the fact that the entire process takes less than five minutes. They claim to have served over 65 million downloads, so to say it is a popular website creation tool would be an understatement. It is reported that 22% of all active domains operate on the WordPress platform.

Here are some "must have" WordPress plugins that I strongly recommend. A Google search for "WordPress Plug Ins" will uncover many more. An extensive list can be found at urbangiraffe.com.

AddThis at: wordpress.org/extend/plugins/addthis/. This plug-in is for social site bookmarking.

Akismet at: wordpress.org/extend/plugins/akismet/. This helps to filter out spam comments if you have set up a comments feature on your WordPress website.

All In One Adsense & YPN at: wordpress.org/extend/plugins/all-in-one-adsense-and-ypn-pro/. This software code facilitates your Google Adsense commission program.

"Lighter Menus" simplifies the rather awkward basic WordPress menu system. Find it at: wordpress.org/tags/lighter-menu-plugin.

Google XML Sitemaps keep Google happy. You definitely want them to like your site. Happy Google, happy you! Download from: wordpress.org/extend/plugins/google-sitemap-generator/. This plug-in also alerts the major search engines whenever your sitemap has been updated.

Tiny MCE Advanced at: wordpress.org/extend/plugins/tinymce-advanced/. This is an enhancement to the WordPress editor.

HeadSpace2 facilitates adding your meta tags (site-identifying code words.) Download from: wordpress.org/extend/plugins/headspace2/.

WP-DB Manager at: wordpress.org/extend/plugins/wp-dbmanager/ is rather important. You DO want to be able to restore and back-up your precious files, no?

WP Super Cache is a very fast caching engine producing static html code files, at: wordpress.org/extend/plugins/wp-super-cache/.

Ultimate Google Analytics are great for all of your statistical analyses:wordpress.org/extend/plugins/ultimate-google-analytics/. This adds a Google JavaScript on each of your website pages.

WordPress Automatic Upgrade is useful for keeping the code in your account up to date. It is found within your account.

Technically (not that it matters!) CaRP (nor CrAP) is an RSS to HTML parser/converter written in PHP. Whatever. You will find the CaRP script for FREE at: geckotribe.com/rss/carp/.

Creating a WordPress blog-based website for book selling purposes is important because WordPress is automatically search-engine friendly. It enables customizable permalinks, meaning that your blog posts automatically contain original descriptive keywords in their page names.

Backlinks, links coming in from other websites to yours, are very important for enhancing your search engine ranking. There is an interesting program that works with WordPress data to help you accomplish getting backlinks. Go to CommentHut at: commenthut.com. Download their FREE "Lite" version. It finds WordPress blog-websites using your chosen keywords and phrases. It only indexes those websites that accept comments. You can even specify that the program only spit out high-page-rank websites which are most important to your search engine optimization.

Visit the websites that the program comes up with and post **relevant** comments on the site. Put your URL link in the "Your Website" panel. When your comment is published, presto, you have your one-way back link! The upgraded (read "pay for it") version expands the search to many more blog platforms other than WordPress. According to their website this gives you 90% more results!

For all of the information you could ever want about WordPress go to: codex.wordpress.org. Prepare to be overwhelmed!

Aside from Blogger and WordPress, there are many other popular blog programs, most of them totally FREE. Be certain to check out:

Tumbler.com, a micro-blog. Easy to use.
Blogetery.com, a WordPress platform.
Typepad.com, very business focused. One of my favorites.
Blogster.com a social-site type community.
Hubpages.com is commercial-oriented.
LiveJournal.com, a social-site-type.
Xanga.com, you get a "site" not just a weblog.
Blog.com, integrates with many other platforms.

Wikispaces.com claims seven-million members.
Tblog.com, a social-site type.

Because they are FREE there is no reason not to try these as well. You might just find they fit your needs even better.

LINKING CONSIDERATIONS

There is a point you need to consider in all of your blog links. Instead of simply using your keyword-rich URL by itself, consider enhancing the link with additional keywords. This requires messing a bit with HTML code, but if you simply can fill in your information in the appropriate code you will be fine (omit the brackets [ ]):

<a href=http://www.[your exact URL]>[your added keywords]</a>

Doing this is a big help in your ultimate goal of high search engine positioning.

You can find "DoFollow" backlink-friendly blog sites at: dofollow.info. Also check out: techtipsmaster.com/do-follow-forums-and-blogs.html, and: robdogg.com/wordpress/2008/02/10/7-high-page-rank-blogs-that-dofollow/

Some high PageRank blogs to which you should definitely post blogs are:

bloglines.com
blogpulse.com
blogdiffer.com
getblogs.com
blogorama.com
blogcatalog.com
blogstreet.com
blogflux.com
bloghub.com

Here are some other websites I would strongly recommend for posting short, concise blog posts that are very content-rich:

reddit.com
stumbleupon.com
xanga.com
ehow.com
digg.com
hubpages.com

You may be amazed at the response you will get from posting at these sites. Great for potential sales, for building your mailing lists, and for generating the backlinks that will help you achieve higher search engine rankings. <u>And remember, all of this exposure is **FREE.**</u>

Remember to close all of your blogs with your link, but make it a "cliff hanger". Don't just say: "To learn more about (your book) click here". Instead, say something like: "(There is one book that (whatever special benefit your book offers). Want to know what it is? Find out at (your website URL or specific purchase page URL)." See the difference? On which link would you be more likely to click?

PODCASTING FOR THE TALKATIVE

Want to **talk** about your book? No chapter on blogging would be complete without mention of a technique called "Podcasting". This is simply a self-**audio**-publishing medium. It is far beyond the scope and intention of this book to give you anything other than a quick overview of podcasting.

If some time in the future you want to get seriously involved in podcasting there are many fine books on the subject you can purchase or borrow from the library.

Podcasts are created by anyone desiring to share some passion or idea with the masses via any listening device. If one has the means to listen to a radio broadcast, they can listen to your podcast, which of course will extoll the virtues of your book's topic. This includes not only portable devices such as an iPod (or any MP3 player), but also any desktop or laptop computer or tablet.

A podcast can be downloaded directly from a podcaster's website and listened to on a PC using any media player you choose. It is a way for people to fill their iPods and other media devices with something other than music!

Podcasts can be scripted or unscripted. They bring their listeners unedited, real, from-the-heart commentary on anything imaginable. As opposed to radio, there are no regulations as to content. It is a Libertarian's delight!

Technically there is a computer language called "XML" (Extensible Markup Language). A text form called "RSS" (Real Simple Syndication) links to an XML formatted file. RSS feeds enable you to share your verbal content across the internet.

One needs specialized software to receive podcasts. This software is referred to generically as "podcatchers" which in techno-geek speak are known as "podcast aggregators". This open-source (read "FREE and ever-evolving") software tool allows you to subscribe to and manage any RSS feeds you want automatically downloaded. Popular RSS feed software for Microsoft Windows includes:

Doppler Radio at: dopplerradio.net/
iPodder   at: ipodder.sourceforge.net/download/index.php
Nimiq at: podcatchermatrix.org/show/nimiq

I suggest you access each of these sites and click on all of the various links. Once you have studied these sites in detail you will have an excellent grasp of the entire podcasting realm.

With podcasts you are able to lie in bed and broadcast to the world about your book and book topic! You decide on the length of your show, and decide how often it will run.

Clearly there is a potential marketing component here. While your visitors are seeking entertaining and informative listening, the opportunity to include a pitch for your book's website clearly exists. But, as with maintaining a blog with frequent fresh content, podcasting can take a good bit of your time.

You should also realize that, unless you can produce a very special and highly-sought podcast on a regular schedule, it is unlikely that your audience will ever exceed a few thousand listeners. This is not a very large potential group of buyers for your books.

In order to produce podcasts you only need a computer, a website, and a microphone, plus some software downloaded from the internet. To be effective your computer should have a Pentium 4 or stronger central processing unit (CPU), one gigabyte of random access memory (RAM), four gigabytes of free space on your hard drive, and "line in/line out" connections for a microphone and headset.

You will need specialized recording software. I believe the most commonly used product is "Audacity for Windows", an audio editor/recorder. You can access this at: audacity.sourceforge.net/. The best part is that it's FREE.

If you already have an adequate computer your only additional cost is a decent microphone and headset from Radio Shack (now called, for whatever idiotic reason, simply "The Shack") or Walmart.
If you want to add podcasted RSS feeds to your website, use a website script CaRP mentioned earlier. You will need a "File Transfer Protocol" (FTP) program to use in conjunction with CaRP. (I use "Cute FTP" at cuteftp.com). A Google search will turn up many ftp programs. Filezilla at: filezilla.com is another popular ftp program.

There are, in my never humble opinion, lots of time-effective (and therefore cost-effective....time **is** money) ways to promote your books on the internet. Perhaps I have not given podcasting a serious marketing effort. I'm told by friends who get their jollies talking into a microphone in their pajamas that podcasting is great fun and can be profitable. I'm just too busy adding to my bank account with other less time-intensive marketing methods.

To summarize: **Be certain you use your primary keyword(s) in your blog URL. Use your primary key phrase in the title of your posts. Use your secondary keywords in the body of your post. Tweak your default settings as described above. Update as often as possible.**

So there you have it. Blogging can be a highly profitable, though a bit time consuming, way to market your books. Google's Blogger can get your marketing website up and running quickly. Pinging will get you noticed quickly. WordPress can make starting a marketing website a breeze. Podcasting is an awareness you can file away for the future.

Take the time to work with blogs and podcasts. You may well find, as many self-publishers have, that it is one of the most powerful ways to promote your books and increase sales.

JUST DO IT!

CHAPTER 22
<u>MARKETING WITH FORUMS</u>

One of the best routes to gaining customers and backlinks is through participation in the forums in your book's niche. In my experience participating in forums takes a great deal of time, like blogging and podcasting, that might be better spent doing press releases and articles, and perfecting a website. But there are many self-publishers who make a great living participating in forums, so don't let me stop you from trying. The best news is that it is FREE!

If you happen to be someone who enjoys social sites such as Facebook and MySpace and love to Tweet on Twitter and Pin on Pinterest, and are on a zero or limited budget, you might just find forum participation to be an enjoyable way to build a valuable focused email list, make sales, and improve your Google PageRank.

Your first step is to locate forums and discussion groups in your book's niche.

Google search is my choice for locating forums. Just Google "(your keywords) forums" and you will usually find more than you can handle. The more specialized your niche the fewer forums you will find, but you will almost always find many more than you could possibly join.

Check out the number of active members, the more the better. Look for forums with lots of active members that have lots of discussions. As you look at various forums the differences will become obvious.
Also a search at: big-boards.com will show you a useful database from which you can derive market intelligence such as the number of members and the member activity in various forums.

Many forums, known as the "DoFollow" ones, will allow you to put your website link in your signature at the end of your post. This can be very helpful in your marketing because the whole idea is for forum members to click on your link just to see what you are all about. Don't disappoint them! Be sure they see a great freebie in exchange for their email address.

So you only want to post with forums that are in the "DoFollow" category. This allows for the prospect of getting those valuable backlinks by sending participants to your website. A good long rated-list of these can be found at : vtechtip.com/2009/10/list-of-dofollow-forums-with-high-pagerank-update-regularly.html.

Some forums to which I would strongly suggest that you post are:

forums.mysql.com
bungie.net/forums/default.aspx
bbpress.org/forums/
flickr.com/help/forum/en-vs/
forum.joomla.org/
forums.cnet.com
forums.feedburner.com/
affiliateseeking.com/forums

webmasterforums.net
htmlforums.com
dnforum.com
sitepoint.com/forums
webhostingtalk.com

There are a number of other very popular forums that focus on a particular area of interest:

AssociatePrograms.com for affiliate marketing.

eWealth.com also for affiliate marketing.

WorkAtHome.com for home based businesses.

MoneyMakerGroup.com about making money.

InternetBased Moms.com for work-at-home moms.

DNSscoop.com is domainer focused.

The best place to put anchor text backlinks by offering comments and advice can be found at: warriorforum.com. Their focus is on internet marketing. Enter subtly: "Did you see that great new 400 page book,,,,,,,,". Get the idea?

Forums can be used for research, subtle advertising, or even some paid advertising banners. Your job is to actively participate in discussions and over time build a presence that will ultimately result in visitors to your book-promotion websites.

Be certain to read each forum's posting rules, and be sure to follow them. Many forums are not friendly to individuals who are openly trying to market their books. You need to invest the time to wander through the various forum topics and determine what participants are asking about the most that may relate to your book's niche topic.

Your general approach in forums needs to be subtle. You cannot appear to be "selling". People want to be helped, not sold. If you see a question your product addresses you could respond to the questioner with something along the lines of: "I saw this answer to your question and I think they can help you with your problem." The underlined portion is your hidden "contextual text link" which takes them to your website or the Amazon or Smashwords purchase point.

You can put a text link anywhere in a short paragraph discussing a relevant topic by adding: "……and I found a report that explains it in detail here." This text link could take them to your squeeze page where they get a free report so you can get their email address for later use in promoting your books. It could take them to a point-of-purchase. Either way, you win!

If you find that you enjoy the forum universe there is an all-in-one platform that you can utilize. Go to ning.com. At this writing they have a free 30-day trial. Beyond that, you are looking at a substantial cost of between $300/year and $720/year depending upon which of their two programs you choose.

Ning includes the whole ball of wax: a hosted website, blogs for you and for your members, email list building and management, marketing to site visitors and members, and discussion forums for infinite discussions. In addition there is every bell and whistle you might ever need to have your own successful forum site.

Although a Ning site could be created within hours, consider this a very long term project before serious book sales income is generated. Properly executed Ning could be an absolute gold mine. It's at least worth a look.

There are five basic approaches to marketing through forums:

ANSWER QUESTIONS. This can work especially well for you if you have a great deal of knowledge on the subject in question.

ASK QUESTIONS. This is a fast way to initiate a stream of forum posts where you can eventually subtly market your product.

ASK FOR AN OPINION: Make a long list of affiliate programs from ClickBank and other networks. Then ask: "Has anyone had any experience with xxxxx". This can start a stream of forum posts.

ASK FOR A CRITIQUE: Write an article in your book's niche, post it in your blog, and ask peoples' opinion of the article. Not only will you learn about your article's popularity, you will be getting involved in that forum. **OFFER THE ARTICLE AS YOU WOULD TO AN ARTICLE DIRECTORY.** (See Chapter 20) Go back to the forum and offer the article (assuming people liked it) for publication, with the proviso that they leave your resource box (at end of the article with your URL or affiliate link) exactly as is.

Regarding "Answering Questions": A rather sneaky trick that many self-publishing marketers employ to promote their book's purchase links is asking a question from one computer and answering the question **themselves** from a different computer! This can get a forum posting string going in a hurry!

Some question and answer sites frequently used in this fashion are:

answers.yahoo.com
groups.google.com
wiki.answers.com
allexperts.com
yeda.com
askhelpdesk.com
help.com
theanswerbank.com

Two **different** computers must be employed. This sort of tomfoolery is immediately caught and deleted if only one computer is used because each computer has a <u>unique identification number</u>. I guess duling-computers technique can work, but don't get caught doing it. Remember, your internet reputation is VERY important. Tricks aside, your participation as an "expert" on Q & A sites can help you build a reputation in your niche and ultimately lead to increased sales of your books.

Click on the above eight sites, and sign up for free accounts. Then study what others are posting and the replies they get. Do not advertise your products in your posts. You will eventually create a "signature" containing your Amazon, Smashwords or website links at each forum. That signature is what does your marketing for you.

In summary, your job is to appear in the forums as a "helpful" person. If it fits, you could even eventually establish yourself as the "resident expert". You must appear to be providing useful advice with the links to back it up. But don't just put links in everything you post until you perceive that people have trust in your prior no-link input.

You certainly do not have to have an all-inclusive solution such as Ning to start a forum, though you might find that approach to be the most time and cost effective way to go. A WordPress website creation program has a plugin that allows you to create your own forums on the WordPress site itself.

Either through Ning or WordPress you can build your own multiple forums on sub-niches which over time can add more and more members to you email list. It is often said that: "The Long-Term Riches Are In The eMail List".

You can also create and start your own forums using programs found at:

vbulletin.com

vbadvanced.com
whoson.com (Live Chat program)

Forum participation, as with blogging, takes time and patience. You might find that this time could be better spent elsewhere. Just remember that forums are yet another one of many different approaches to marketing your books.

Good luck, and Happy Posting!

CHAPTER 23
<u>DIRECT SALES AT EBAY AND CRAIGS LIST</u>

One of the ways you can sell your books effectively is having an "eBay store". It's a "virtual" brick and mortar store! Properly run it should cover many times the cost to own it, and be a significant source of book sales.

Having your very own eBay Store, when properly conceived and created, can be a huge money-maker. It isn't exactly inexpensive, but of course cost is only relative.

In total, including the monthly fee, if you were to sell a <u>single</u> $9.97 book from your store it would cost you around $17.35…not a great way to make money! (eBay takes an 11% final value fee for each sale). But TEN sales of that same product would only cost around $27 and show a return on investment of 200%, not at all bad. You can expand the arithmetic from there, but it is clear that if you can sell many of an item the cost of the store and final value fee become irrelevant.

The big advantage to having an eBay store is the fact that you can list as many books as you like, one, ten, a hundred, or a thousand! And you can sell those auction-banned downloadable ebooks without being forced to create physical CDs.   You see, eBay has made it impossible to sell your virtual product in their auction format. The only way around that is to convert your books to CDs, which are OK be sold in auctions.

As with all eBay advertising, there are a host of "enhancement fees" that can be added and are worth considering but are not absolutely needed to attract buyers. Having an eBay store gets you access to advanced design, marketing and reporting features. It also assures you the lowest Fixed Price listing fees, substantially lower than in the auctions.

By far the most important aspect of having your own eBay store is the fact that you can send the search engines, or any other traffic source, directly to it just as you would with any website. When you consider that your auctions last at most ten days and the items in your store are perpetually there to be bought, the advantage of having a store becomes quite obvious.

On top of that, customers who arrived to buy one item might very well view and buy other items from your potentially-limitless store inventory. Plus you now have the ability to offer freebies or send newsletters telling buyers what promotions you are running and what new books you will be offering. If you employ the "Good 'Till Cancelled" option an item will automatically re-list every 30 days or until you cancel the sale.

Sales are shown to improve when you create an **"About Me"** page. Putting a "face" behind an anonymous offering makes many bidders feel more comfortable. Make it an attractive face, preferably female. <u>Both men and women prefer to buy from women.</u> Don't ask! I'm not a shrink.

When writing your personal profile do not exaggerate or make yourself seem like more than you are. You want a brief snapshot of who you are, how and why you got into selling on eBay, and why they want to deal with you.

Take advantage of eBay's "Store Referral Credit". If you can send customers to your eBay store from your website or other outside link, and they buy something from the store inventory when they arrive, you get a full 75% off your Final Value Fees for every item bought!

Keep in touch with the reality of the many scams to which you could fall prey. Check out eBay's "Trust and Safety Discussions Board". Also periodically look at: pirsquare.letzebuerg.com.biz/scams.html.

When using an eBay Store or eBayClassified ad, never send your downloadable book .pdf file via email. Instead send an email directing the buyer to a site where it can be downloaded in a .zip format. (Use the FREE .zip tool at: winzip.com). And if at all possible register for eBay's "ID Verify" service. This just costs a few bucks, and you may need to make a few inexpensive token purchases. This will help establish your credibility with buyers.

NEVER accept payment for anything in cash. Even if the buyer sends it by Registered Mail you may receive an empty envelope from a buyer who swears there was money in it when posted. It is OK to accept payment by Cashier's check or money order, though these are relatively easy to counterfeit. In general, using a PayPal account for all things eBay is best, if for no other reason than the fact that eBay owns PayPal!

The above techniques are used by every successful eBay entrepreneur I know. It may look like a lot to learn, but after a while it becomes second nature and very simple.

CRAIGSLIST:

Let's look at the well-known "Craigslist". This was the brainchild of a San Francisco computer programmer named Craig Newmark. A single guy, he wanted to keep track of what was going on in his home city. After letting a few of his friends in on it, the idea became a viral sensation! The area of focus became the entire Bay area. It became an internet bulletin board, with evermore categories added. Soon other cities wanted "in", and the site expanded nationally then internationally. It became a place for people to offer their services, hire employees, meet other people for discussions, and buy and sell various items. It has evolved into a very powerful marketing tool for your earning pleasure!

Many internet marketers are discouraged by the Craigslist culture. Members who contribute to the community bulletin board police the "Rules", some written, some not. Any member can complain about an advertiser and Craigslist will remove the ad. Craigslist's community is chock full of anti-capitalists who see themselves as champions of anti-commercialism and will complain about any ad that they feel might be, God forbid, for profit! You see, Craigslist is NOT in the ad/marketing business. They are a sort of ".org" non-profit group community bulletin board as opposed to a commercial marketplace.

But advertising here is a "numbers game". According to their website they get twenty BILLION page views a month! More than fifty million people in the United States use Craig's List. That's one in six Americans! (More like one in four if you take kids out of the calculation.) They have almost a hundred topical forums on the website, and claim one-hundred-twenty-million monthly forum postings. Each month they get *fifty million* new free classified ads. These are massive numbers.

You have two possible approaches to earning on Craig's List, direct advertising, and forum participation. Let's look first at direct free advertising. For starters, set up an account at craigslist.org (not .com). Just fill in your email address, copy the anti-fraud symbols shown, and click "Create Account". You will be sent an email message with a special link. Click on the link and you are taken to a page to create a password. Do so, and "Bingo!", you have an account. You do not actually <u>need</u> an account to post ads, but it is helpful in keeping things organized. It is also needed to access details of forum posts.

Spend some time carefully searching all of the categories and subcategories available to you and choose some subcategories that relate to one of your niches. There are so many choices it should not be difficult to find matches. Incidentally, running the same ad (with very different wording) in different subcategories exposes it to entirely different universes of potential customers. (If you run exactly the same or closely-similarly-worded ad it will probably get removed as a rules violation brought to the attention of Craigslist by the army of self-appointed censors.)

You will be asked to choose a city for display of your ad. It takes a bit of time to hit all of the individual major markets, because you need to go through the entire posting procedure time and time again. And here again you need to re-word your ads for each post lest the anti-capitalists score again. The good news is that it only takes a couple of minutes per city. And you can even go for international markets!

Strictly by the rules you are NOT supposed to post multiple ads in different categories, or ads in more than one city. You are not supposed to be a professional marketer selling anything! The site is intended for rank amateurs selling "yard sale" and "garage sale" stuff. This is why you need to carefully study other ads that are being run and get a feel for what does and does not pass muster.

Properly worded, you should at least be able to direct individuals to your website to sell them something, squeeze-page them into collecting their email address, or have them click on a publishing platform link. Just learn the Craigslist culture well and you are on your way to placing profitable free ads any time you choose.

The second approach to marketing on Craigslist is through their forums. The Craig's List forums are sort of a free-for-all, with lots of threads completely off topic. But there seems to be no rules regarding posting website URLs and publishing-platform links, which makes your job easier. And being free makes it painless!

My suggestion is for you to check out Craigslist forums on something close to your niche. They have forums for "fitness", "food", "garden", "money", "health", "sports", "music", "pets" and a host of others. Try to see if you can find logical places to post short blurbs about your product or your affiliate offers with appropriate links. I've done this, and gotten some click-throughs and revenue. This is not always a huge moneymaker, but it is pretty darned easy cash.

OTHER ADVERTISING SITES TO CONSIDER

Aside from Craigslist, which many consider a pain to use, there are many other classified ad sites that are worth using as well.

You can find a long list at: thefreeadforum.com/ads/page/list-of-high-traffic-classified-ads-websites.html.

Here are some I suggest you use:

The number 2 classifieds site behind Craigslist is backpage.com. This site is primarily for sexually oriented material, so you probably won't use it. Then again.............

Kijiji.com will take you to eBayClassified ads

Gumtree.com is a busy UK classified site. Do not overlook such English-language sites that happen to be located overseas.

Classified ads.com is an English-speaking world-focused classified site.

Inetgiant.com is a great place to advertise your green products.

Adpost.com is an international site with a mostly English-speaking audience.

Adlandpro.com has very busy business opportunity and pet sections.

Classifiedadsforfree.com is a well-organized worldwide site.

Pennysaverusa.com/classifieds/usa/index.html is the online version of the old *Penny Saver* newspaper.

Epage.com has been in business since 1994, which tells me something positive. It even pre-dates Google! You get excellent exposure here
because of their large affiliate program.

Recycler.com is an easy to use classified ads site.

Webcosmo.com is US focused but with opportunities for overseas ads.

Hoobly.com has had 15,000+ people have clicked their "like" button, so they must be doing something right!

Freeadlists.com is US based and very comprehensive.

Sell.com probably has one of the most valuable domain names in existence! In business for over a decade, it gets great exposure.

Bestwayclassifieds.com is a fast growing site with decent traffic.

Choseyouritem.com if nothing else has a very high opinion of its own site! Worth listing here.

Wantedwants.com also consider themselves to be the best in the world! Decent traffic and worth posting ads here Freeclassifieds.com is a mobile-device friendly site worth listings.

Businesslist.com/post-classified-ad/ is a US targeted classifieds site. All your ads are automatically tweeted to their twitter account.

Theworldwideclassifieds.pressmania.com/ has the feature of having never -expiring ads. Free ads get live links and even the ability to add a YouTube video to your ad.

Blujay.com is worth a long look. They submit your ads to Google Product Search shopping, which opens your offerings up to massive traffic. And you get a free online store to list all of your products under one roof if you so desire.

Ecrater.com, is very similar to BluJay. It also gets placement in Google searches. Title and word your ads to be rich in key search terms and you have a good chance of making sales at zero cost to you. They also provide a free store for you to stock. Create free advertising on "Yahoo!Classifieds" through the Yahoo!Directory at: dir.yahoo.com/business_and_economy/clas sifieds/. Obviously they get massive traffic, and keyword-rich ads with the right headline will get seen. Go for it!

Ablewise.com will place your free ads worldwide! (Ten countries listed, mostly English speaking). They claim over 128,000,000 visitors!

Internetbusinessmoms.com has blog posts and forums that can be used for subtle advertising

Inetgiant.com offers free classifieds with a paid alternative that claims a 20x better response. Try it for free.

Adlandpro.com will run your classified ads for free. Study their site.

ClassifiedAds.com is location-specific, which can be limiting (though you can run the same ad in large metro areas using different accounts.) Here again, nothing ventured nothing gained. Check it out.

Backpage.com gives you a massive number of choices for you to pin-point match ads to your potential customers.

Nationwidenewspapers.com offers access to a massive number of all sorts of publications that accept classified ads. They do not specifically offer free ads, but some of their ad packages are inexpensive and offer great exposure. Well worth a look.

Homebusinessmag.com is a widely circulated magazine dedicated to franchise offers and all manner of home-business opportunities. You can pay for their ads, both display and classified formats, but it is possible to get freebies if you meet certain criteria. "Free Listings are reserved for companies that offer substantial home-based businesses" or so states their website. If you have such a book, go for the freebie.

There are over a hundred-fifty specialized article directories which you should not overlook. These cover a massive range of niches. For example, if your book relates to dogs you have: bestdogarticles.com. Targeting golfers? Try: golfmastery.us.

Horseback riding? See: horsebackridingarticles.com. Google the term: "Specialist Article Directories" for a list, or just try surfing for (your niche) articles.com and see what pops up!

One of the other FREE sources of traffic to view your affiliate ads are "Traffic Exchanges". You simply enter your website domain name or an affiliate link and it will be displayed in rotation with other members of the traffic exchange. Here are the three I find best, though as with any major topic in this ebook doing a Google search will turn up many others.

TrafficSwarm at: trafficswarm.com offers free website traffic and free ads in their website directory.

HitPulse at: hitpulse.com offers free unlimited traffic to you book ad websites.

InstantBuzz at: instantbuzz.com states on their website: "This breakthrough new patent-pending advertising technology <u>will</u> <u>send targeted visitors to your site</u> *today*. That's right. Install it right now (it's free and takes only a few seconds), and we'll start sending you targeted high quality traffic to your site today. Not tomorrow. Not next week. *Today.* 100% FREE - Installs in Seconds." That sounds like an offer that you can't refuse!

The free classified advertising sites are all absolutely flooded with ads, but you cannot beat "FREE". It is up to you to make your ads better than your competition's ads, or to write ads in niches where there is little or no competition.

Just look at free classified advertising as another of the many possible multiple streams of internet income. Over time your various streams can flow together to create a massive river of book sales profits!

Free (and paid) classified advertising is by far the easiest way to promote anything you are selling. Whether it is your book in electronic or printed form, or a CD of your book exposing it to targeted buyers for little or no cost simply cannot be beat. Adhere to this one business model and profits are sure to follow!

JUST DO IT!!!

CHAPTER 24
<u>DIRECT SALES</u>
<u>ON YOUR MINI-WEBSITES</u>

There is a type of website known as a "mini-site", that can be a maxi-profit-center for selling your books. A "mini-site" is a one-page website comprising a headline, sub-headline, a one-product sales letter, and an action button. Alternately, they can also be set up to have a few very short niche-focused articles and up to three pages.

They are quick to make, a few hours at most, simple to construct, and makes book sales and list-building very fast. Because they are so easy to create some internet marketers have a hundred or more mini-sites with different books and reports, each earning a few dollars a day. Do the math. This can create a huge income over time.

These sites are not to be confused with full-blown websites such as those described in Chapter 21. These mini-sites are not intended to get high ranking in Google.

There are intended to be a presence to which you can drive paid traffic using a program called Google AdWords.

If you have no ideas for a topic about which to write, just find any popular niche (a niche is focused interest). Go to: google.com and search "Google Keyword Tool External". Key in subjects that interest you. Google will provide you with suggested keywords and phrases. Chose keywords and phrases that have a minimum number of sites competing against you for those keyword phrases (called "long-tail keywords"). To determine this figure, just enter the different keywords and phrases between parentheses "xxxx" at google.com.   The number of sites competing for those keywords appears at the top. Anything under 25,000 is a winner (for common terms the figure will be in the millions!)

Decide on the topic for your book. Then write, buy, have ghostwritten, use public domain, or get a private label product, to produce at least three short (300 words is fine) keyword-rich articles.

Create a landing page, or squeeze page if you want to try to create a mailing list. On a squeeze page you offer some incentive, a free report, newsletter, etc., in exchange for a visitor's email address.

One quick and easy strategy is to buy a domain name based solely on your book's key words. Then create a simple one-page site with keyword-rich content and add the link. Nothing else. Then drive traffic with Google AdWords pay-per-click program described below, in addition to the other ways suggested in Chapters 17 – 23.

One good place to access simple, easily created mini-site templates is: diyminisite.com. Try creating a few niche-focused mini-sites, and when you see the results you can obtain with relative ease you run the risk of becoming a mini-site addict! It's fun and profitable.

Using Google AdWords pay per click advertising, the same as with using Google's Blogger platform (Chapter 21), will get your site indexed quickly. But if you choose to do neither you can still get indexed quickly.....for a price.

The Google website has a form on it for you to fill out that is meant to tell Google that your website exists. **NEVER** fill out this form! If you do that and nothing else it will take four to six weeks for them to index your site. This is also true about the forms found on other search engines.

There is, however, a way to get indexed in 24 hours! You simply purchase a backlink from a Page Rank 7 website. This can often be rented for a month for under $200. Once you are indexed you can cancel the link. Is it worth it? Perhaps. What is six weeks of potential traffic to your book-selling site worth to you? Hard to say.

There are companies who broker backlinks. Check out:

Text Link Brokers at: textlinkbrokers.com
Link Adage at: linkadage.com
Text-Link-Ads at: text-link-ads.com

Somewhere FAR down the road if you can create a website that eventually earns a Page Rank of 6 or 7 you can make a lot of extra money by selling <u>your</u> backlinks. This is just another of the many possible multiple streams of internet income that could happen ancillary to selling your books..

Now here is my biggest secret: <u>You can have a mini-site</u> created for $5.00! That's right folks, for just five bucks there are many individuals that will build you a one-to-three-page mini-site.
Once again, **<u>THINK FIVERR</u>**! Just go to fiverr.com and enter "build me a website" in the search window. Many fiverrs do this well and often overnight.

It is up to you to provide the text for the site, a copy of your book's front cover, and any company or personal logo. The fiverr website-builder needs your domain name. You need to provide the code that PayPal (who you will be using to collect payments) gives you. You will provide the .pdf file of your book for buyers to download once they buy it, if they choose to do so from your website. You will provide the links that take the site visitor directly to your purchase link at Kindle, Create Space or Smashwords. You need to provide the "About Author" file.

After providing the above information it will be at most one to two days before you get a completed website file to upload to your host server!

You will need to buy a domain name (at godaddy.com or wherever domains are sold), and select a web host (such as oneandone.com or wherever else websites are hosted). Then you will need to drive traffic to the mini-site with Google AdWords.

GOOGLE ADWORDS

The most common approach to buying traffic is "Pay Per Click"

marketing (PPC in the trade, also often referred to as "CPC" or "Cost Per Click"). It is extremely powerful.

What is amazing about PPC advertising is that you can:

Pin-point target your potential customers;

Tailor what your visitor sees to their exact interests;

Drop the visitor off exactly where you have placed the offer that matches their interest;

Pay only when they get to see your offer;

Accurately measure your results;

Set a "do not exceed" budget;

Run ads 24/7/365 with zero supervision!

Overall, PPC marketing does all the things more "traditional" advertising does, but does it faster and in general more cost effectively, plus it adds the benefit of easily measurable results.

You must become familiar with the key PPC resource links. This is where you buy your paid advertising. Go to, and search through, the following:

Google Adwords site at: google.com/adwords;

Yahoo! Search Marketing site at: searchmarketing.yahoo.com;

Microsoft Ad Center at: adcenter.marketing.com.

For now, focus on Google Adwords only. This platform is classified-advertising nirvana! Compared to off-line advertising it is far more focused, and a lot less expensive. For lower cost your promotions are targeted to the very people who are interested in your book. This contrasts with off-line ads where only a few readers might even notice your ads at all, let alone give a hoot.

In 2000 Google decided to take full advantage of its strong brand and created the automated self-serve advertising program they named "AdWords". (The idea of paid search engine advertising had been pioneered a few years earlier by a company called "GoTo", later named "Overture" and ultimately acquired by Yahoo!)

It is far easier to set up an AdWords campaign than any offline advertising because everything takes place at a single focused website location. And there is virtually no time delay to wait for results. I have seen an AdWords ads score hits within **minutes** of publication! Pay to play. And earn.

There are many hundreds of millions of Google search visitors every day. Google-searching has become habitual for many (such as me), and it is reported that the average United States user averages over three Google searches daily. I probably average twenty!

Google complicates your overall AdWords experience a bit with various algorithms used to evaluate the relevancy of your website which they compare to the actual wording of your ad. They also factor in the percentage of people who actually click through to your website, and will even disable ads that show very low click-through rates.

So, though it is essentially an auction-for-position platform, you cannot be 100%

certain that a given bid will provide the expected placement.

Your AdWords account has three components, your "Account", your "Campaigns" and "Ad Groups". Your account is associated with your unique email address, password, and billing information. Your campaign is where you choose your daily budget, geo-targeting, and any ending date. The ad group, which can contain multiple ads, is where the ads are created and your keywords chosen.

ADWORDS PRICING

The "daily budget" you set is not carved in stone, unless you click on the "Recommended Budget" link and see the message "Budget is OK". Google wants a budget that, according to their algorithm, will "max out" the times your ad appears when your keywords match the search keywords. It is a good idea to accept their suggestion. If you do not there is no guarantee that your stated budget will not be exceeded. They want you to make money, but they want to make their share too!

In theory you can use hundreds of keyword phrases within your AdGroup, but you will make a lot less work for yourself by finding and using __ten__ or so phrases that narrowly target your niche. This makes it far easier for you to track which ads work best with which set of keywords.

I have found that my click-through rate increases if there is an **EXACT** match between a word in my book title and the phrase the user typed in. Not only your ad title but your ad body **MUST** contain relevant keywords. Try to run five to ten sets of ads that match closely to the keywords in each group.

Note that Google prohibits what they call "double serving". If you happen to have multiplebooks that are all relevant to the same keywords you cannot have more than one of them showing up on the same page of search results. This prevents a creative advertiser from crowding out the competition by dominating all of the choice positions.

In writing your ads follow good "AIDA" principles (Attention, Interest, Desire, Action). Google is not exactly generous with the space you are allowed.   You get 25 characters for your headline, and 35 characters for each of the two lines in the ad body. The "Display URL", your web address the user sees below your ad, is also limited to 35 characters, but that should be no problem.

The "Landing URL", which must send visitors directly to the information sought without a second click, can be 1,024 characters. This allows you to use whatever extensions and tracking codes you might wish to add to your display URL.

Your ad may very well result in an "Editorial Disapproval" email! I've gotten my share.

You have somehow violated one of Google's written, implied, or seemingly made-up-on-the-fly regulations. Violations of minor editorial rules are common. Things such as unnecessary punctuation, misspelled words, all capitals, and capitalizing the first letter of each word in the ad are all no-nos. It isn't worth the time and effort to disagree with their finding and try to convince Google to allow your ad to show as written. Just clean it up and move on. They rule. You don't.

Ads can get immediate results, but there is a Google ad-review process which can delay the appearance of your ad. This delay could be a week or more if you are using very popular keywords, or your ad is placed at a time (such as Christmas) when lots of ads are under review. Always allow for a few week's delay.

There are three major syntax forms available to you within your AdWords account. Study and learn these:

EXACT: The user's entry must exactly match a word or phrase in your keyword list. You force exact matches by entering your keywords between brackets ([xxxxxxx]). (The [ ] are unnecessary with single keywords.) The more words in an exact match the better targeted the user will be, but the number of visitors are fewer in proportion to the number of words bracketed.

PHRASE: Putting quotation marks ("xxxx") around a phrase will trigger your ad when that exact phrase appears somewhere in a user's search. It does not matter what other words a user might enter in the search preceding or trailing the chosen phrase.

BROAD: Keywords entered without any punctuation will trigger your ad if they appear anywhere in the user's search.

Only your own experience with your ads over time will dictate how syntax-focus relates to the success of a particular book-sales campaign. There are no hard and fast rules because there are so many possible variables. Just test, record results, and optimize over time.

Do a Google search for any keyword term. Check out the first four websites that come up and then go to the AdWords Suggestion Tool , enter a keyword at: adwords.google.com/select/keywordtoolexternal. The program will suggest related keywords. You can also click on "Site Related Keywords" where you can enter an actual website address, and Google will suggest keywords based on that address.

For your website domain name, follow the book title as closely as possible. This would be something like: "makebigbucksfromhome.com", where the title of your book is "Make Big Bucks From Home".   If the .com version is unavailable, you could try the .net or .org version. Alternately, you could make a minor change in the URL such as

"makebigbuckfromhome.com" or
"makebigbucksfromhome1.com".

If you want some FREE ideas for a domain
name to register for a particular keyword or
keyword phrase in connection with an
affiliate campaign go to: 123finder.com.
Enter your keywords, up comes a list of URL
ideas. Useful site.

Keyword research is critical to your success
(See Chapter 11).
What you hope to find are relevant keywords
that have significant search volume for
which you are the **only** bidder and can buy
for the minimum $0.05 per click. The more
such phrases you can weave into your
account the better your return on investment
should be.

It pays to snatch the low-hanging keyword
fruit first. Getting into a bidding war for a
single common term makes no sense at all.
You can readily bid small amounts for
multiple obscure-long-tail-keywords that will

in combination generate more traffic for a lot less money! This is a very important concept to grasp. It is why many people fail to be satisfied with their AdWords results.

The big mistake many newbies make is to list too many keywords in their AdWords campaign. They'll spend $50.00, see $30.00 income, and consider the item a loser, drop it, and go on to another book. What they fail to do is to analyze which keywords produced that $30.00 profit. Very often it is one or two out of twenty. No-brainer. Drop non-performing 18 keywords, focus a second sum on the two winners, and the chance of achieving a fine rate of return is excellent.

There are certain useful nuances that can be applied to keywords. These include:

Plural vs singular form;

Verb forms and related nouns (e.g., repair, repairing, how to repair);

Common misspellings (e.g., weeding for wedding);

Hyphenated vs non-hyphenated words;

Abbreviations (e.g. wkly for weekly);

Acronyms (you are allowed to put these in all capitals);

Phrase questions preceded by who, what, where, when and why.

On one hand Google is very easy to use and to start PPC advertising. On the other hand there is a fairly steep learning curve if you hope to maximize your Google AdWords results and not throw away cash.

Google AdWords has a valuable tool called "Traffic Estimator" that shows how much you would have to pay to get the number one position for a given keyword or phrase. You can access this without actually running a PPC campaign.

Set up a dummy campaign with an obscure term. 1. log in and "create a new campaign". 2. Create ad group "TEST" Headline TEST, descriptions TEST. 3. Enter a single keyword. & save it.   When you click "Calculate Estimate" Google will now tell you the dollars it will theoretically require take the top position. To be sure the dummy ad never runs put in very low bid (as a secondary preventative safety) and "Pause" the ad forever.

OPTIMIZE YOUR PPC ADS

You optimize your ad wording by "split testing". Using this technique you try variations of your headline and text such as: "Free Widgets Fast" (get your widget NOW); "Order Free Widgets" (order today for fast delivery); "Compare Widget Offers" (don't just buy but compare available offers); "Free Widget Offers Reviewed" (here's what I think of widget offer a, b or c). Get the idea?

Because you are paying for **any** click it doesn't matter on which of these split-test ads someone clicks. Over time, looking at your visitor statistics you will be able to tell which wording works best and focus your entire budget on paying for clicks for that particular ad.

Never pre-assume which ad and headline will work best. Personal intuition doesn't cut it. My gut feelings on a given ad are usually proven wrong by split-testing! You will very often be amazed to see one wording pulling five times the clicks of another for absolutely no obvious reason. Just test, test, test.

If you see a competitor's ad at the top of the Google results day after day, (when you enter a particular keyword or phrase) week after week, and know they are paying a high ppc rate, you know they are either crazy (and enjoy losing money every day) or they are making money at the ppc rate they are paying.

It is a bit of a chore to track one or more competitors' sites on a daily basis, but needless to say there is a company out there who will do it for you.....for a price. This valuable resource to access is at: spyfu.com. They maintain a database so you can go back a month and see who has been bidding on what for how long. This is a great way to see whether your competition is making money with ppc without it costing you a dime!

One VERY important last thought in your PPC ad writing. It is a key tip that has been shown time and time again to increase clicks. It is called the "Cliffhanger". **EVERY ad copy, that the web-surfer (potential buyer) sees, should be seen closing with "and ...." as if the ad were cut off by the character restrictions. It is human nature to want to learn "and WHAT???"** It has been shown by split testing to increase clicks. Easy, and very important to do.

Skill in advertising creation and placement is vital to your success in selling your books. Of course you can have the perfect ad and generate oodles of clicks, but if visitors do not take the desired action on your landing page. This is true whether that action is providing their email address in exchange for a freebie, direct linking to your book offer at Kindle, CreateSpace or Smashwords, or buying your .pdf file directly. No action at all, and your click- payment was wasted. That is why your website landing page is the single most important aspect of your overall internet book marketing campaign.

There are a few useful rules to follow as you evaluate problems that might occur during your AdWords campaigns:

If certain keywords show very few clicks, drop them at once.

If you are getting insufficient clicks overall, it is possible that traffic does not actually exist for those keywords. It is also possible that you have a really bad ad, too few keywords, or too low a position in the search engine (below three or four) for anyone to ever see your ads.

If you get lots of clicks but low or no sales your landing page sucks. Perhaps your offer sucks too.

If your clicks are too costly, lower your bid gradually to see how it affects your ranking position. Perhaps Google doesn't like your site and hasn't told you yet (the infamous "Google Slap"). If you see a sudden big hike in your click costs delete the ad group and start from scratch. If your new ad is disapproved, delete it and try again. Don't argue.

If you get a "Final Warning" for something take it seriously, suspend the campaign, and make logical changes. It is always a good idea for your wife or partner to have a backup account!

If your excellent click-through rate suddenly plunges, search your keyword terms and see if someone decided to copy your ad. It happens.

If your impressions and clicks drop suddenly you may have been the victim of the dreaded aforementioned "Google Slap", which is best avoided by following their rules closely. Just follow basic good website practices and you will be rewarded by Google with lower click costs and higher search positioning.

There is a very clever way to mitigate your PPC advertising costs. Once you have a successful website getting lots of PPC traffic that you can document you can sell advertising space on your website to offset your PPC bid costs.

You will need to show your average Cost Per Click (CPC) rate (under $0.05 is great), high Alexa rank (under one million is great), Google page rank (4 or better is fine), and your average or previous day's page views. And of course your ads need to show up at or near the top position for your chosen keywords.

Once you know your average cost for your PPC ads on a monthly basis, divide by the number of ads you choose to sell to get a good idea of your "break even" point in pricing your ads. Ads on a great site can easily be sold for $97 a month and possibly a lot more. It is a good idea to offer proportionally lower daily, weekly and two-week rates as well.

Even if you find you cannot cover 100% of your ppc ad costs, you can certainly lower your costs dramatically and greatly increase your return on investment. Remember, simply cutting ad costs in half doubles your advertising ROI!
Selling five to ten ads should do the trick. Preferably these should be text ads, because banner ads are proving to have reached the point where people seldom click

on them. You can try selling both, but you will have happier and longer-term advertisers if you steer them to text ads.

Use unsold space for your own ads. Don't overwhelm your own primary offer with other's paid ads. You can set your page up so that your book offer or offers clearly dominate.

To get visitors to purchase your ad space, simply include something on your website that stands out and shouts: "HOT!! Your Ad Could Be Here For Just $3.13 A Day!!! Reach Google's 100-Plus Million Daily Buyers!"

You may be very pleasantly surprised to find that you not only cover your PPC costs but can actually turn a profit that could end up exceeding the profit from your book offer! Free traffic is wonderful, but the majority of successful self-publisheing entrepreneurs are reported to have found that PPC advertising, cost-mitigated or not, over the long term is their best route to internet riches and a massive stream of alternate income sources.

AVOIDING FAKE VISITORS

At some point in time you may encounter a problem with computer generated "visitors" trying to join your email list list or access your information or fill out some form on your website. As you surf the web you will come upon many websites that have solved this problem with a type of "challenge-response" test called "CAPTCHA".

This is an acronym for "Completely Automated Public Turing test to tell Computers and Humans Apart". It consists of a line of text contorted in a way that a human can read (barely) and copy it and a robot computer cannot. Free CAPTCHA plugins are available at: captcha.net.

WHAT ABOUT TARGETING OVERSEAS MARKETS?

If you happen to be bi-lingual you are in luck! You can vastly expend your market, save money on translations, and earn much more selling your books to a non-English-speaking set of buyers.

Most Europeans speak as many as three or more languages fluently. That is seldom true with Americans, who seem to have enough trouble with English!

When you are beginning your book marketing adventure, focusing on English speaking countries is all you need to do. Somewhere done the road if you want your entire website (or even some book or report) translated into a foreign language, you have two choices.

The correct way is to hire a professional translator. This can be very expensive, but with your guidance it can create an end result that will offer a satisfactory experience for your overseas buyer.

The wrong way, in my never-humble opinion, is to use one of the on-line translation programs that are available. You can TRY:

Babelfish.altavista.com
Translator.go.com
Dictionary.com/translate/
Voila.com/services/translate/

Of course, you can always take a crack at fiverr.com. Although it will cost you five dollars for a given rather small number of words, you still may find it to be a cost-effective way to reach a large audience beyond the United States, Canada, Australia and New Zealand. The three most universally understood languages aside from English are Spanish, French, German, and Italian. Obviously there are far more people who speak some Chinese dialect, but whether they would be interested in your particular book, or have the facility to buy it, is problematic!

If nothing else readingany poorly-translated website creates great comic relief for your overseas visitors! You never know. You just might make a sale or two out of pity. Mostly you will just look as an idiot.

Having your own website gathering email addresses and selling your own books is the classic business model that has made more self-publishing entrepreneur millionaires than any other. It may not be the easiest of the marketing methods to establish, but it is a sound, long-term business model that can create an enormous residual income for life.

CHAPTER 25
ADVERTISING KEYS

EBAY CLASSIFIED ADS

When most people think of eBay they think "auctions". There is no question that the eBay auction paradigm can be used very effectively in internet marketing of physical items, such as CDs of your books. We also spoke earlier about establishing your own eBay store, which is a very good idea.

But there is a lesser known way for self-publishers to cash in on eBay that has nothing to do with auctions. It is called "eBay Classified Advertising". It is GOD'S gift to the book marketer! It can be used to generate direct sales, and to build a massive mailing list.

Advertising off-line, in magazines and newspapers that accept classified ads, can often be very profitable and should not be overlooked. The problem here is that all but the smallest off-line ads are quite costly, so most use the minimum-size two-line ads to generate leads. These ads are priced by the word, offer little in the way of "selling", and are generally squeezed together with dozens of competitors' ads.

EBay Classifieds, on the other hand, can be huge and bold and include hundreds of words and many pictures. An equivalent size off-line ad would be prohibitively expensive, hundreds if not thousands of dollars. The eBay cost? Zero for "local classifieds", around $10 for a 30-day exposure across the entire eBay site!

The KEY to using eBay Classifieds profitably is the fact that these ads respond to searches made by eBay shoppers **who you can target 100% with your keywords!** Everyone searching for your type of book is a potential buyer. Your job is to create a **KEYWORD RICH AD**, starting with the title of the ad.

With eBay Classifieds there are no final selling fees to eat into your profits. And probably most important there is no "feedback" provision which precludes the habitually-unsatisfied or outright- fraudulent buyers from leaving negative feedback about you and your books. Unfortunately there exists a universe of idiots out there in cyberspace who get their jollies castigating innocent sellers just for the fun of it.

Most of the successful eBayers I know use this classified ad format to effectively build their mailing lists. They offer a free report and send the visitor to a website where they sign up for the freebie. But the visitor can also be directed to Amazon or Smashwords purchase link, or even buy your book directly from your website, killing two birdies with a single rock! There are many others who skip this multi-step process, which admittedly takes more time, in favor of simply sending the visitor directly to the book's purchase buttons. Personally I use both.

A word of caution. eBay "Rules" can be very confusing and ambiguous, and even worse, change frequently. What is true today is not necessarily true tomorrow. As pointed out above, for years fortunes were made selling digitally-downloaded books through eBay auctions until this was outlawed.

To check on eBay's latest rules, go to: pages.ebay.com/help/sell/f-ad.html. It is a good idea to click on everything and read it all. It takes a few hours but could save you serious grief.

Also do the same at: pages.ebay.com/help/policies/listing-links.html. Irrespective of the "letter of the law" it is quite apparent from all of the ads on eBay that they do not rigorously enforce their restrictions. Pull up lots of ads and see this for yourself.

It is a good idea to check out other classified ads to see what eBay is permitting (or turning a blind eye towards, rules-against notwithstanding) at any given time. If you see many ads doing exactly what you want to do (e.g., sending visitors away from eBay to non-eBay email-boxes or to Amazon or to your own website or email autoresponder) it is a pretty safe bet you can do the same.

Under "What Is Not Allowed On eBay Classifieds" is a list of almost fifty "no-nos". Read it, and abide by it. This is actually a pretty good list for you to follow in all of your internet book marketing, because most of the items would be prohibited in any platform you might choose.

I have no personal moral problem marketing "nude art books" as long as it is non-pornographic, but apparently eBay sees all nudity as bad. If that is your genre look beyond eBay.

You can post 25 local ads per day, all FREE! Each ad can be posted in only one category, and in only one chosen ZIP code.

Posting that many ads daily, and doing it properly, is quite a chore. You could end up posting 750 ads a month and even then it is quite unlikely that you would not generate a significant income!

There also exists in eBay a different level of Classified ad that is not quite free but offers some serious advantages. This is running Classified Ads directly on eBay.com. If you access pages.ebay.com/help/sell/formats.html you will see a detailed comparison under "Selecting A Selling Format".

In this option you state a price, the buyer contacts you, and you handle the transaction directly outside of eBay, for example, on your website.

Most ads run for 30 days, although there is a "Good Until Cancelled" option. Either way you are charged a small "insertion fee" every 30 days. The fees charged are based on the category of product selected. You are

NOT charged a final value fee, primarily because eBay has no idea how many of something you have sold.

These classified ads on eBay are a **serious** bargain! Each 30-day period presently costs only $9.95. The first picture in the ad is free. This would be your front cover. Additional pictures cost only $0.15 each. There are a number of "upgrades" that can add, for example, an additional $6.10/30-days, or $16.05 ad cost total. This is still a major bargain over off-line classifieds. A big ad with ten pictures keyword-targeted to a specific niche audience costing under $18.00 is a real bargain.

The upgrades are intended to make your ads stand out in a crowd. I can't make a very strong argument for using upgrades, because it is the wording of your title and your ad that drives most visitors to your site, but using them can't hurt either.

With eBay Classifieds you can sell on any eBay country site regardless of where you reside or from what country your eBay account was initially registered. Just note that fees and allowable products do vary country to country. Digital products are the most relevant example of this. They are AOK in the UK but a no-no in the US of A!

The same is true for outside linking. In reality you will find some ads running with outside links. So join the crowd until such time as eBay decides to tighten their rules or better police them.

Many marketers will post classified ads linking to their own paid-for listings on eBay. They set up identical Classified Ads ending by the hour and linked to the paid-for listing giving the product a high profile. Though you are keyword-limited to 55 spaces in your eBay BuyItNow titles, you are not limited in putting keywords and phrases throughout your classified ads. **You want to appear at**

least once for a large number of search terms.

EBay sales are proven to improve when you create an "About Me" page. Putting a "face" behind an anonymous book offering makes many bidders more comfortable. Make it an attractive face, preferably female. Both men and women prefer to buy from women. Don't ask! I'm not a shrink. It is the reason why many male writers use female pen names.

You can put virtually anything on this page, including a link to your website. The only restriction here is that any products you offer on your website that you are **also** selling on eBay must be priced $1.00 higher than on eBay auctions.

If eBay's "Rules Of The Moment" are not permitting payment links in your classified ads use an opt-in form in lieu of a payment button. When the buyer opts in with their name and email address, they click on a bar that says: "Click To Receive Ordering

Information" that takes them directly to your payment page. There is almost always a "work-around".

You also will be collecting names for your email list, and for anyone who does not order your book you can email them to get them to reconsider!

Regardless of costs and restrictions selling through eBay Classified Ads represents perhaps the single best internet book marketplace. Promoting your book's website using eBay Classifieds to drive traffic is by far one of the easiest and most cost-effective ways to earn a very significant self-publishing income.

FREE ON-LINE CLASSIFIED ADS TO ENHANCE PROFITS

Now here is a real NO BRAINER. It costs exactly zero run your book ads on free classified advertising sites. Nothing. Nada.

So why not go for it? No reason whatsoever.

By far the most useful FREE advertising site is: usfreeads.com. They have been providing advertising services for over a decade. What makes this site special is that you can link to your website or ebook publishing sites directly from your ad, a **HUGE** plus.   Not all ad sites permit this.

Running free classified ads to promote your books is by far the easiest and most cost effective way you employ to generate income. JUST DO IT!

_____

CHAPTER 26

<u>WHEN WILL I BE RICH?</u>

Understand this up front: You cannot <u>expect</u> a huge amount of royalty income from any *single* book title. Of course there are exceptions to this. You might come up with a one-in-a-million super-best-seller, but the odds are strongly against that happening. <u>Your success will depend far more on your own **marketing skill** than on the quality of your books themselves.</u>

Many very mediocre books sell very well because they are marketed very well. Never lose sight of the fact that the average intelligence of the average buyer is not in the genius category!

You should consider earning $20/month/title from Kindle to be good. Add in Smashwords and CreateSpace and combined $50/month/title is quite possible. Ten titles, $500/month is realistic. One-hundred titles? How about $5,000/month! **This is a pure**

numbers game. How quickly you can publish material is entirely up to you. It is reported in major media that some self-publishers are getting quite rich, becoming millionaires, with 1,000+ titles!

This is a "set it and forget it" business model. It is reliably reported that some individuals make in excess of $30,000 a month selling simple inexpensive how-to reports on Kindle. One lady who I believe writes gothic fiction has been written up in national magazines as having earned well over two million dollars from Kindle alone! Remember, at zero out-of-pocket cost to you the biggest and most powerful book marketing company in the history of the world, Amazon, will bend over backwards to help you sell anything you can produce in writing! Then they pay you up to 70% of the retail price you set, 100% of which is profit for you! And they keep marketing your item forever!!! This is an absolute NO BRAINER.

Amazon helps with exposure, does all of the customer billing, and provides marketing that would take the average internet marketer years to perfect. You simply provide them with the digital ebook or report content and they periodically send you royalty checks! Awesome!

Once you begin to publish books, **DO NOT GET DISCOURAGED BY SLOW EARLY RESULTS.** In fact, you can count on them. It could take a month before sales start to materialize. DO publish at least five books before you worry about getting results from the first book. Or better yet twenty-five! It is not as hard as it sounds once you get the hang of it. At some point in time you must begin your own marketing blitz.

As I said above, over time there are some self-published authors who have hundreds, even thousands, of titles in their publishing-platform accounts and earn a fortune! The important thing to remember is that every title remains in these programs **forever**, so it just becomes a matter of compounding results.

My personal goal is to try to double my self-publishing revenue every month. I base this on the simple math behind old bet where the loser readily agrees to pay the winner a penny each day and then double it each day for a month. On the face of that it seems like you are risking very little. Not quite!

Take that one penny and double it every day for a 31 day month. Can you guess how much money you will have? It is unlikely your guess will be close! After week one you'll be up to a staggering $1.28! By the end of week 2, almost half way home, you're up to $163.94, not exactly life-changing.

But by the end of week three, almost done (?) we have a nice tidy $24,192.32. Not a retirement fund, but not exactly chump change either. But guess what? At month's end, just 31 days after we started with a penny, we have just under twenty-five-million dollars ($24,774,039.84 to be exact)!!! I never cease to be amazed by this simple exercise in arithmetic.

This is why my goal is to double my revenue every month. If this means I have to produce a two ebooks a day and post them to my accounts then so be it. Never lose sight of the fact that a saleable short ebook or report can be created in a couple of hours once you get into the habit of doing them.

Incidentally, people who buy Kindle ebooks have seven days to return them. Do not concern yourself with buyers requesting refunds. Yes, there are "Refund Bandits" out there. Fortunately there are **far** more honest buyers. You can expect around 1% to 2% refunds, **irrespective** of your material quality. Of course, if your material is truly awful you can expect many more refunds and some pretty ugly comments.

<u>The main thing is to stick with the program</u>. This is not a get-rich-quick system. But it is a way to create, over time, a residual income stream that can be counted upon indefinitely!

NOTE: If you are interested in making a living as an entrepreneur in internet commerce, and in learning the possible multiple streams of internet income that can be earned in many ways other than self-publishing, please look on Amazon (or any ebook platform) for our latest book: ***"Money By Internet: How To Get Started Making Money Online".*** You can also buy the print edition at Amazon as well. There is no other book available today that covers virtually **all** of the many ways that anyone can earn money from home using their computer. And we purposely made this huge volume very affordable so that as many people as possible can benefit from it.

ALSO RECENTLY FROM LIONS PRIDE PUBLISHING

"Reverse Mortgage Dangers" written by a heretic reverse mortgage loan originator!

"The Black Belt – How To Do Karate (The Art of Personal Self-Defense)" with a Forward by Great Grand Master Aaron Banks.

"Making Money From Domain Names – The Domain Flipper's Bible", for work-from-home income.

ABOUT THE AUTHOR

There is one very logical question you should ask: "Who are you and why should I listen to what you have to say?" It is a very valid question.

I'm going to resist the urge to show you copies of my bank statements, as many "internet gurus" are so fond of doing. These are just too easy to fake or embellish or show out of context to have any credibility.

Suffice it to say I have been rather successful at internet commerce far longer than most, since 1995 in fact. During that time I have made it a point to learn as much as I can from all of the biggest names in internet marketing, and to apply that knowledge to my book publishing. I didn't invent the e-commerce wheel, nor did I try to re-invent it along the way. I simply learn as much as I can as often as possible from those rare pioneers who blazed the trail to internet and self-publishing riches.

With over a hundred books and countless articles to my credit, my goal is to eventually publish at least 600 books to surpass the number written by my role model Isaac Asimov!

My proudest literary achievement to date was being chosen to write for *Leaders* magazine, which is only distributed to Heads of State and corporate CEOs!

I was born in a slum called Bedford-Stuyvesant (known affectionately as "Bed-Sty") in Brooklyn, New York. The hood was an interesting mixture of immigrant Italians and Irish, Protestants, Blacks, and Hassidic Jews, about in equal proportions. Both of my parents worked two menial jobs just to put food on the table. I had no siblings, and no educated role models. My birth year was 1938. Yep, I'm an old poop in his mid-seventies! Surprised? (And I'll probably have to live to 110 to pass Asimov in published volume!)

I was a typical "street kid", frequent truant, pool hustler, shop-lifter, and survivor in a neighborhood where survival was both an art-form and a not-always reality. My best and only real skills were survival and shooting pool, the latter providing sustenance cash. Back in those days today's recreational drugs were almost unheard of. Had I been born in the modern era I might well have ended up a junkie, in prison, or dead.

My first job, at age eight, was delivering staggering shoulder-hung loads of dry-cleaned clothes for a local cleaner. My first "real" job was packing and shipping bottles of arthritis pills for a defunct company called Dolcin, under the ever-watchful eye of the meanest lady that ever lived, my wretched first boss the evil Sheila. She was the direct descendant of a long line of slave drivers!

What happened between then and a decade or so ago I won't bore you with. I had the usual nine-to-fives, learned a lot from the school of hard knocks, suffered through two divorces, and served in the Army as a grunt during Vietnam. I more or less raised three kids. I never quite made the "big time". During a "religious period" I even became an ordained minister! But after a succession of failed business attempts, in 1994 I found myself in Chapter 7 bankruptcy and penniless.

Fortunately I had by then married my third wife, an exceptional and beautiful young lady who certainly didn't marry me for my money! She always believed in me, often more than I believed in myself. I'm thrilled to say we are soon to celebrate our 30th Anniversary! She is one of a kind.

Post-bankruptcy, from reaching up to touch bottom, today we live in absolute paradise on a twenty-acre ranch bordering millions of acres of State lands in the High Sonoran Desert in sunny southern Arizona with our two great pups. We have a beautiful 5,573 square foot stone home, have travelled the world, and have every creature comfort we could ever want.

What could conceivably have happened between a 1994 bankruptcy and today? From Chapter 7 and reaching up to touch bottom to total creature comfort? <u>INTERNET COMMERCE AND SELF-PUBLISHING HAPPENED!</u>

Some internet visionaries began to emerge, and some were willing to share the money-making knowledge they had learned through long and tedious trial and error. Internet "wealth seminars" proliferated. In the late '90s I made it a point to attend every seminar I could, all around the country. I always made certain to meet the "guru" running the classes and try to pick their brains clean. Some were late teenagers, half the age of my kids! Some were geniuses. Some were clearly out to make a fast buck. But all had useful lessons to be absorbed. I was a willing sponge.

Today I have no pressing need to continue my daily self-publishing work. I believe it was Samuel Clemens (Mark Twain) who first said: "Make your vocation your vacation". I really enjoy doing the tasks that are needed to earn money as a self-publisher of books on the internet. I plan to do it forever. With an occasional trip to Paris thrown in!

If I can help others, especially the unemployed and under-employed to improve their lives, so much the better. If I can interest seniors such as myself in supplementing their retirement incomes through writing that would be wonderful. Can I make life easier for stay-at-home moms and dads? I hope so. If I can show college students how they can reduce their loan debt I'd feel quite good about that as well.

Personally, regardless of how much money I earn selling books it will never be enough. My dreams of creating an enduring charitable foundation to fund a worthy cause will require as much as I can ever earn. I need quite a few internet millions to make a real dent in this project. It's a five-year plan. And it will happen.

To summarize, I have over the past decade-plus participated in every phase of internet commerce I could find. I know that any of it can be profitable, but I have also learned which methods are most cost effective for me, and which I found could be implemented the fastest. **I can save you years of time and tend of thousands of dollars by sharing with you what I have learned through years of publishing trial and error.**

I hope this book will provide you with the knowledge you need to begin your quest for internet wealth through book publishing. There is absolutely no reason for you not to give this wonderful journey a try. Good luck, and GOD bless!

APPENDIX

<u>WRITING RESOURCES</u>

So you would love to self-publish but don't believe you can write? Forgedaboutit! You can actually learn to become a very credible author. It just takes a bit of study and learning and practice. Remember what I said earlier: You are not trying to win a Pulitzer Prize or create a best-seller with your first book. Both could come in time, but for now producing average material for an average audience is all you need to do to start making money.

Two words of caution. **<u>NEVER</u>** be tempted to sign up with any company who, either for a fee or a piece of the pie, will "help" you "get published". I have personally had experience with a number of these, as have many of my author friends (especially before the digital age), and we found them all to be totally worthless. You **CAN** self-publish if you follow the how-to material in this book.

Second caution: Do not get bogged down with an overload of how-to-write material. You can easily end up with the "paralysis of analysis".

For starters there is a wealth of excellent writing information at the publishing sites described earlier in this book: Amazon Kindle at kdp.amazon,con; Smashwords at smashwords.com, and Amazon printed-books-on-demand at createspace.com. Study all of these before you look any further for a learning experience. There is really little else you need.

I personally learned the **basics** of writing from a fine gentleman named Dan Poynter, who I visited in person some years ago. I've also attended his seminars. His website: parapublishing.com is a must-visit. His book: *The Self-Publishing Manual* , which he updates frequently, has been my writing bible since 1979! I haven't actually re-read it in almost a decade, but it definitely inspired me to continue my self-publishing back in the frustrating pre-electronics days.

Incidentally, not a single word in this book you are holding was extracted from Poynter's book, unless by an accident of memory! His approach is quite different from mine.

THE AUTHOR (glasses) WITH DAN POYNTER AT ONE OF DAN'S SEMINARS

There are many books in print relating to learning to write. One book in particular stands out in my mind as by far the best ever written on the subject. I believe it is out of print, but perhaps you can find a copy through your library or eBay. This self-published book, written by Dr. Jeffrey Lant, is: *How To Make A Whole Lot More Than $1,000,000 Writing, Commissioning, Publishing And Selling "How-To" Information.*

For an extensive list of internet writing resources go to: dmoz.org/arts/writers_resources_.

There are a number of other websites I suggest you take a look at, listed alphabetically:

blurb.com (they even have free writer's software) My niece has created coffee-table photo-books using their platform. I have never considered it a source of money-making text-only books.

bookemon.com This is an interesting self-publishing site that may be worth exploring.

booktango.com   This is a publishing platform that appears similar to Smashwords. They take zero dollars from your retail price, that is, your royalty is 100%! If I have learned nothing else in life it is that there is no such thing as a free lunch. I'm not certain exactly how they derive their revenue, but to date I have not explored publishing on their platform.

bookwritinghelp.com This site has the best assortment of free articles on writing of any I have found.

enhancemywriting.com They bill themselves as "A Complete Collection Of Indispensable Writing Resources". Lots of useful stuff there.

everywritersresource.com   An interesting site worth exploring.

kunaki.com (if you want to sell spoken-CDs of your book) In my mind Kunaki is one of your best sources of internet income, if you have the time to verbalize your books. For an extremely low price they will create a professional-looking CD in a wrapped jewel case with proper inserts and send it to your buyer. Especially if you have a website, you can sell these at many times your Kunaki cost. You can also sell them at Amazon Kindle Direct Publishing.

writersresources.com There are lots of interesting free articles available here.

Of course you have virtually unlimited material to rework/rewrite through Private Label Rights and Public Domain material.

Never forget that if you want to pay for original reports and even complete books there are freelance writers at fiverr.com, elance.com and rentacoder.com who will ghost-write for you. Whether going this route is cost-effective is questionable, but if you don't mind spending the money you might want to try this route at the beginning of your budding writing career.

The main thing is **GET STARTED.** Self-publishing, above all else, is **FUN!** The fact that you can earn a very fine income pursuing it is a **significant** added benefit.

GLOSSARY OF INTERNET AND PUBLISHING TERMS

The following are the more commonly used internet terminology with which you should become familiar. If you come across a term not defined here, Wikipedia.com is always my first choice for a definition.

AFFILIATE: An individual who markets another's book for a percentage of the proceeds. Certain platforms, such as Smashwords, have an available affiliate program within their platform. You can always register with clickbank.com and offer your book at a percentage split upon which you decide.

AUTHOR PAGE: The various publishing platforms provide you with adequate space to tell about yourself, and to list other books you have published.

AUTO VETTER: AutoVetter is Smashwords' proprietary technology that automatically scans your uploaded ebook and reports back to you about potential formatting problems.

AUTO RESPONDER: A computer program that detects the receipt of an email and automatically replies to the sender with a pre-programmed response.

BACKUPS: Data from you that your Web hosts copy (typically once a day) in case of a loss of data situation. Backups allow hosts to easily restore lost data. Be certain your host offers backup.

BANDWIDTH: The amount of information transferred both to and from a website or server during a prescribed period of time. This is usually measured in "bytes". Hosting companies generally offer packages that come with different bandwidth transfer limits per month.

BISAC: "Book Industry Standards and Communications" is the standard book category coding system. You will find drop-down menus in the publishing platforms that offer you these choices.

BLOCK PARAGRAPH: When paragraphs are not indented, but are stretched from one side of the page to the other, that's a block paragraph. It is generally accepted that "right justified" is more readable for the viewer.

BLOG HOSTING: These are special scripts that let users automatically post new information to a website.

BLOGOSPHERE: The sum of all information available on blogs.

BPS: Stands for **B**its **P**er **S**econd. It is a measurement of how fast data flows from one place to another. A 56K modem can move about 56,000 bits per second.

BROADBAND: Refers to internet connections with much greater bandwidth than possible with a dial-up modem.

BROWSER: (or "Web Browser"): A computer program used to view and interact with the content of Web pages on the internet.

CLIENT: A software program designed to contact and obtain data from a server. For example, a Web Browser is a kind of client.

CO-LOCATION: When a user owns his/her own Web server, but houses it in the hosting provider's facilities for easy management, a high-speed connection, security, backup power and technical support, said user is "co-locating".

CONTROL PANEL: A Web-based application that allows you to manage various aspects of your hosting account. This includes uploading data and files, adding email accounts, changing contact information, installing shopping carts and/or databases and viewing statistics

COOKIE: A piece of information sent by a Web Server to a Web Browser that forces the Browser to save the information and alert the Server whenever the Browser makes additional requests from the Server! It is used by vendors to keep track of a computer user's surfing history.

COPYRIGHT: (Not "copywrite".) A copyright is the exclusive legal right, normally held by the author of a book, to copy, adapt or distribute their creation. Often a publisher will control the copyright. Wikipedia has good technical descriptions found under "Copyright" and "Authors' Rights".

DEDICATED HOSTING: When you rent or lease your own Web server that is housed at a hosting provider's facilities for easy management, a high-speed connection, security, backup power and technical support, you are buying dedicated hosting.

DIAL-UP: A method of connecting to the internet using telephone lines. It is very slow compared with other "high-speed-internet" and "wireless" connections.

DISCOVERY: This is an important term used in ebook publishing. It describes how "findable" your book is by a prospective buyer. The key is **proper categorization.** You want people to find your book whether or not they are specifically looking for it! This is why it is so important to publish across as many different publishing platforms as possible.

DISK SPACE: The amount of space available for you to house your website files on your host's server.

DOMAIN NAME: An address assigned to a website for identification purposes that can be translated by a domain name server into a server's IP address that includes a top-level domain.

DOMAIN NAME SYSTEM: Keeps a database of domain names and their corresponding IP addresses, so that when a user searches for a domain name, the request can be routed to the server where the desired website resides

DOMAIN REGISTRAR: A company responsible for managing your domain names and helping you secure the rights to a specific domain name you wish to purchase.

DOWNLOAD/UPLOAD: This refers to electronically getting a file from an internet location "down" to your computer, or sending a file from your computer "up" to an internet site. You "upload" your files to your publishing platforms.

DRM: This stands for Digital Rights Management, and is offered as an option by some publishing platforms. On the surface it sounds like a good idea. It is "copy protection" technology designed to prevent piracy of your work. It makes it harder for someone who has bought your book to print or duplicate it. The problem with DRM is two-fold. First of all, a dedicated book pirate can easily bypass DRM. But more important it restricts your reader from enjoying your book on different devices. Although I have never "split tested" to see whether DRM helps or hurts my bottom line, conventional wisdom is to never employ it.

EBOOK: This is a generic term for any book offered electronically, intended to be read on portable devices or downloaded from a website.

EPUB: This is an open industry standard ebook format It is the format used almost universally, with the major exception of Amazon Kindle which does not support it.

EPUBCHECK: This is an EPUB validation tool designed to automatically determine if an EPUB file is compliant with the EPUB standard. Many ebook platforms require its application to your book's manuscript to insure that your book will appear on customers' devices correctly. You can learn more about it at:
code.google.com/p/epubcheck/.

FAQ: Stands for "Frequently Asked Questions." All publishing platforms offer this collection of questions that have been asked by publishers in the past. Studying the entire set of FAQs will often answer every question you might have about a particular publishing platform.

FILE TRANSFER PROTOCOL (FTP): A commonly used method for exchanging files over the Internet by uploading or downloading files to a server. (An example would be "cuteFTP".)

FILENAME EXTENSION: A tag that appears at the end of each file name. It consists of a dot and then three or four letters that signify the type of file and format.

FIRST LINE INDENT: This is a style of printing your manuscript in a word processing program such as Microsoft Word. It refers to indenting the opening line of every paragraph a few spaces to differentiate it from the next paragraph. Personally I never use it.

FORMAT (noun): This is a reference to a particular electronic program. There are many different ebook formats specific to particular reading devices.

FORMAT (verb): It is used in the context of how you prepare your file in a particular way before uploading it to a publishing platform.

FTP (FILE TRANSFER PROTOCOL): The method of moving information files between two internet sites.

GIF: Stands for **G**raphic **I**nterchange **F**ormat. It is a format used for image files, especially those with large areas of the same color.

HOST: A computer on a computer network that is the repository for services available to other computers on that network.

HYPERLINK: This is a clickable line of text that takes a reader elsewhere. It can be an internal hyperlink taking the reader somewhere within the book itself, as with the "clickable" table of contents. An external hyperlink takes the reader to a site outside of the book, such as your website. To create a hyperlink highlight the text, right mouse click, and select hyperlink. From the

Word panel that appears on the left side chose internal or external.

HYPERTEXT MARKUP LANGUAGE (HTML): The cross-platform language in which the majority of Web pages today are written. Codes are interpreted by Browsers to be properly formatted for visitors. It is relatively easy and helpful to learn, but not entirely necessary.

HYPERTEXT TRANSFER PROTOCOL (HTTP): This is the primary protocol for transferring and receiving data on the Web. It involves a browser connecting to a server, sending a request that specifies its capabilities and then receiving the appropriate data from the server in return. (In general you do not need to type http:// in to your browser before typing in the domain name.)

INDIE AUTHOR/INDIE PUBLISHER:
"Indie" is an abbreviation for "Independent", and is synonymous with "Self-Published. These are the many writers, publishers, and writer-publishers today who have come to recognize that they need neither an agent nor a traditional publishing house to successfully market their books.

INTERNET: This is the huge collection of interconnected networks that are connected using the TCP/IP protocols. It connects tens of thousands of independent networks.

INTERNET PROTOCOL (IP): Sets of rules and regulations agreed upon internationally for all internet functions.

INITIAL CAPS: (as opposed to ALL CAPS): "Caps" is short for "capitals". Initial caps is where the first letter of every word is capitalized. Generally articles of speech such as "the" "this" or "and", and prepositions such as "over" or "on" are only capitalized if they are the first word.

ISBN: Is the acronym for International Standard Book Number.
It does NOT convey copyright. It is a digital identifier that helps second-parties (publishers, retailers and distributors) to identify your particular book to track it or communicate with others about it. It is 100% unique to each specific version of your book.

MANAGED HOSTING: A system whereby you own or lease a server that is located with a service provider. All of its management needs are taken care of by on-site personnel beyond your need to input or control anything.

MEATGRINDER: This term is proprietary to Smashwords. It refers to their software that takes your .doc file once it is properly formatted and converts it to all of the other formats required by the various ebook readers.

METADATA: This is every piece of information that pertains to your particular book. It facilitates your customer finding your book. It includes everything from your title and cover, the ISBN, your book description, your biography, the category classifications, and your price.

METATAG: A specific piece of HTML coding that contains information not normally displayed to the visitor. They are typically used to help search engines categorize a web page.

MOBI: This is the format used by Amazon Kindle, as opposed to EPUB. It is also called a .prc file. (This has nothing to do with the .mobi top-level URL extension.)

NCX: This is short for "**N**avigation **C**ontrol File for **X**ML". It is the Table of Contents summary that accompanies a book presented in EPUB format.

NEWBIE (NOOB): A new or inexperienced internet commerce or self-publishing person.

NUCLEAR METHOD/OPTION: This is a term coined by Smashwords for a system by which an author can strip out Microsoft Word's various unintended glitches. It creates a "virgin" copy of your text from which to begin proper formatting.

PDF: This is short "**P**ortable **D**ocument **F**ormat". It is a .pdf format created a decade ago by Adobe Systems. It is a fixed-layout format that freezes the layout of a book and its word positions. It is the standard for books sold on websites and downloaded by purchasers to their computers. It is not compatible with ebook readers.

PREMIUM CATALOG: This is unique terminology used by Smashwords. It refers to the set of publishing platforms outside of Smashword's own store. To be included in the "catalog" you must upload very specialized file formatting in accordance with their massive "Style Guide". (Think Fiverr!)

REFLOWABLE TEXT: Electronically delivered books, ebooks, are formatted very differently from printed books. While print book text is rigidly fixed, reflowable text can shape-shift across any size reading device screen. This can be anything from a huge computer screen to the smallest iPhone. Readers can alter the font size and spacing to suit their personal needs.

RETAILER: This is the company that sells your ebook directly on its websites, such as Amazon or the Smashwords store.

ROOT SERVER: Servers containing software and data necessary for locating name servers containing authoritative data for top level domains.

RTF: This is shot for Rich Text Format. It is a format that permits any word processor to open your book, and allows manipulation of the fonts before printing (something that a .pdf file does not permit).

SEARCH ENGINE: A system for looking up information on the web. (Google is the best-known search engine.)

SEARCH ENGINE OPTIMIZATION (SEO): This is the practice of designing websites so that they rank as high as possible in search results made on search engines.

SECURE HTTP (SHTTP): An HTTP protocol that uses encryption to protect the traffic between the Server and Browser.

SERVERS: These are specially- networked computers that handle client requests including Web pages, data, email, file transfers and more.

SHARED HOSTING: A system in which multiple clients and websites share a single server. Each account has specific limits on how much space they get and how much data they can transfer. This is the most basic and affordable type of hosting. The downside is if one client manages to crash the servers you go down with them!

SHOPPING CART: Software that lets website visitors select, add and remove products and pay for them online. This software can automatically calculate extra price considerations, such as tax and shipping. It then sends all of the information to the merchant once the transaction is complete.

SIDELOAD: This refers to copying a file directly from your desktop or laptop computer hard drive, or a flash drive, directly to an electronic reading device.

SITE BUILDER: An application offered by most hosting service providers. It allows you to create a website from scratch based on predesigned templates without requiring knowledge of HTML. The finished sites then run on the host's servers and can be accessed and used through any Web browser.

SMASHWORDS SATELLITES: This is a series of narrowly focused ebook sites operated by Smashwords. They are intended to facilitate buyer search by narrowing their search parameters.

STATIC IP: A unique and unchanging IP address given to a website by the hosting provider.

SUBDOMAINS: These are third-level domains, addresses that replace the typical "www". This sends visitors to special URL (i.e. subdomain.website.com) that requests data from a different directory within the original website.

SUPPORT: Technical help provided by Web hosting companies, usually via phone or email, to correct any problems that customers may encounter.

SURFING: The act of looking for information on the web.

TABLE OF CONTENTS: Often referred to as the "TOC" it provides the reader with a summary of your chapter headings. In ebooks this TOC must be formatted in such a way that a reader can click on a chapter name in the TOC and be taken directly to the start of that chapter.

TCP/IP: Stands for Transmission Control Protocol/Internet Protocol. This is a suite of software protocols universally used by every kind of computing system.

TELNET: Standard internet protocol for accessing remote systems, such as Web servers

TOP-LEVEL DOMAIN (TLD): The domain name element to the far right of the address (i.e. .com, .net or .org).

TRAFFIC: The data being transferred over a network, typically between the Browser and Server

UNIFORM RESOURCE LOCATOR (URL): This is your "domain name". It is the standard for giving the address of a resource on the World Wide Web that makes up your Web page's full unique address using alphanumeric characters.

UNMANAGED HOSTING: This is a system whereby you own or lease your own server and are fully responsible for the management of it. This includes troubleshooting, maintenance, applications and security, and is not recommended for anyone who is not an industry professional.

UPTIME: The amount of time in a 24-hour period in which a system is active and able to service requests. Most hosts claim 99%+.

VIRALITY: This is a term with its roots in biology (i.e., viruses). It describes the spread of any data across the internet. This can be through word of mouth, or word of **mouse**! All of the social networking platforms, Facebook, Twitter, MySpace, Pinterest, YouTube or whichever can, " as a virus can spread across the population", spread the word (both good and bad) about your book across the internet. Forums also do this as well.   Many substitute the words "Auto-Effective Marketing" for "Viral Marketing" because of the negative implication of a virus!

WEB HOSTING: This is the service that provides a physical location, space and storage, connectivity and services for websites that allow your files to be accessed and viewed by internet users. Sites are created and then uploaded to a Web hosting service provider's server. Some services provided include email addresses, free site builders and databases, among many other things.

WIKI: This is a kind of website within which the content can be edited and altered from the web browser in which it is being viewed.

WORLD WIDE WEB (WWW): Often incorrectly used as a synonym for "the internet". It is the universe of all web servers that serve web pages to web browsers.

###

www.ingramcontent.com/pod-product-compliance
Lightning Source LLC
LaVergne TN
LVHW022301060326

832902LV00020B/3202